"For the last 30 years I've worked on some of the world's largest events from mass participation running and cycling events to the Olympics. It's always a challenge to get a big event to engage with a large audience – this is one of the few books I've ever seen that distills powerful ideas and strategies that I know have an impact."

Chris Robb, CEO and Founder of Spectrum Worldwide and CycleAsia

"This book contains powerful ingredients and delicious recipes for succeeding in your business. Savour it!"

Pete Evans, Chef, Health Coach, Entrepreneur

"After building an international retail business in three countries with over 1,000 locations I understand the pressure businesses are under to grow and scale. This book is perfect for an entrepreneur, leader or marketing manager to perform at their best."

Julia Langkraehr, Founder of Retail Profile Europe Ltd, Bold Clarity Ltd and international speaker

"I've launched and sold over $5 billion worth of products and I know that successful product sales requires a unique approach. This book shares ideas that will increase your sales and scale your business."

Kevin Harrington, Celebrity Entrepreneur (Original Shark on Shark Tank)

"I read *Oversubscribed* and found myself nodding and reflecting upon success stories that I know or have been a part of. Principles that would take a decade to learn through trial and error are spelled out clearly in this book. Daniel Priestley continues to cement his position as one of the most perceptive, influential, and also, entrepreneurial commentators on the planet."

Andrew Griffiths, Australia's #1 business author, Inc.com featured columnist, CBS Entrepreneurial Advisor

OVERSUBSCRIBED

How to get people lining up to do business with you

Daniel Priestley

CAPSTONE
A Wiley Brand

This edition first published 2015

© 2015 Daniel Priestley

Registered office

John Wiley and Sons Ltd, The Atrium, Southern Gate, Chichester, West Sussex, PO19 8SQ, United Kingdom

For details of our global editorial offices, for customer services and for information about how to apply for permission to reuse the copyright material in this book please see our website at www.wiley.com.

Wiley publishes in a variety of print and electronic formats and by print-on-demand. Some material included with standard print versions of this book may not be included in e-books or in print-on-demand. If this book refers to media such as a CD or DVD that is not included in the version you purchased, you may download this material at http://booksupport.wiley.com. For more information about Wiley products, visit www.wiley.com.

Designations used by companies to distinguish their products are often claimed as trademarks. All brand names and product names used in this book and on its cover are trade names, service marks, trademarks or registered trademarks of their respective owners. The publisher and the book are not associated with any product or vendor mentioned in this book. None of the companies referenced within the book have endorsed the book.

Limit of Liability/Disclaimer of Warranty: While the publisher and author have used their best efforts in preparing this book, they make no representations or warranties with respect to the accuracy or completeness of the contents of this book and specifically disclaim any implied warranties of merchantability or fitness for a particular purpose. It is sold on the understanding that the publisher is not engaged in rendering professional services and neither the publisher nor the author shall be liable for damages arising herefrom. If professional advice or other expert assistance is required, the services of a competent professional should be sought.

Library of Congress Cataloging-in-Publication Data

Priestley, Daniel.
  Oversubscribed : how to get people lining up to do business with you/Daniel Priestley.
    pages cm
  ISBN 978-0-857-08617-4 (hardback)—ISBN 978-0-857-08619-8 (paper)
  1. Marketing. 2. Customer relations. 3. Small business—Growth. I. Title.
  HF5415.P65927 2015
  658.8—dc23
                                                      2014048155

A catalogue record for this book is available from the British Library.

ISBN 978-0-857-08617-4 (hardback)   ISBN 978-0-857-08619-8 (paperback)
ISBN 978-0-857-08623-5 (ebk)   ISBN 978-0-857-08618-1 (ebk)

Cartoons: Andrew Priestley
Cover image: ©iStock.com/denis_pc
Cover design: Wiley

Set in 11/16pt AJensonPro-Regular by Thomson Digital, Noida, India
Printed in Great Britain by TJ International Ltd, Padstow, Cornwall, UK

DEDICATION

For Aléna and Alexander

CONTENTS

Contents

INTRODUCTION

There are restaurants that people line up for. There are products that you must pre-order months in advance. There are tickets that sell out on the day they are released. There are stocks that go roaring up in value right after they float. There are cars that were bought before they were built and properties that sell off the plan when they are nothing more than a set of drawings. There are consultants who are booked six months in advance and hair stylists who charge ten times more than others. There's furniture you can't buy, only pre-order, and bottles of wine that are purchased while their grapes are still hanging on the vine.

There are people who don't chase clients. Clients chase them.

In a world of endless choices, why does this happen? Why do people line up, pay more, and book so far in advance when other options are easily available? Why are these people and products in such high demand?

This book explains why. It's caused by a phenomenon known as being "oversubscribed".

A product or brand reaches a level of being oversubscribed when there are far more buyers than sellers. It's when demand massively outstrips supply. It's when many more people want something than capacity allows for. This book is designed to give you a recipe for becoming oversubscribed, and introduce the underlying ideas that drive this phenomenon.

But before we delve into these concepts and suggestions, it would probably be a good idea to give some background on why you should listen to me. Let me start by telling you a story.

My company runs large business and leadership events around the world. We don't use typical conference rooms in typical hotels; we host our events in theatres and auditoriums that are normally used for popular musicals and shows. What's more, our events are premium priced and oversubscribed – despite the fact that most companies struggle to get 50–100 people to turn up to a free business event.

For example, in January 2013, I issued an email to clients in Sydney, Australia that said: "We have sold too many tickets to the event that you've booked in for. The venue holds 700 people and we've now sold more than that and we have a waiting list forming. If you'd like to sell your ticket back to us – or for any reason you can no longer attend the event – please email us, and we will buy back your ticket today for DOUBLE what you paid for it."

As I mentioned, most business events in Sydney are free, don't get more than 100 attendees and are run by people who live in Sydney and have access to local contacts and networks. Our event was brand new, priced at the top end – and we didn't have a single staff member on the ground in Sydney at that time.

The email wasn't a joke, a gimmick or a ploy. It was genuine. We had sold too many tickets to our event. We had a similar problem in Melbourne two weeks later, then in London, then in Florida.

This wasn't happening by accident. It was orchestrated to be like this. And this book will show you how it's done.

My business often books clients three months in advance. We don't do it to be difficult; it's just the amount of time people need if they want to work with us. If someone says they aren't sure about working with us, we don't argue or try to hard sell them. We smile politely and say that it's OK not to. We don't need to convince people – there are others lined up, waiting.

I launched my first company in 2002 at age 21 with a $7,000 credit card. It was a boutique marketing company specializing in event promotions in the financial services industry. Within 12 months I'd made over $1 million in revenue and had over $300,000 cash in the bank. By age 25, I'd used the same insights to make over $10m in sales and had made myself an enviable amount of money for a young man. Along the way, I discovered some very valuable ideas on how to make a product or service oversubscribed.

At age 25, I moved to London with my best friends and business partners. We launched a new business with a small amount of start-up capital and once again made millions in sales within 12 months. At age 29 I wrote my first book and used the ideas set out in this book to send it to the #1 spot for business books on Amazon. I've raised millions of investment capital for my businesses and helped charities to raise hundreds of thousands of dollars in a short space of time by using the ideas that I will share with you in the pages to come.

As you'll discover as you continue to read through this book, there's no scarcity in the world for people who share abundantly. One of the ways I keep myself oversubscribed today is by the very process of sharing big ideas. I've come to discover that the more I share, the more people demand.

I also believe that the principles in this book lead to better businesses for everyone involved – for the customers who get a higher level of service, for the business owners who stop chasing and for the employees who enjoy working for a company that's in demand.

My vision and hope is for millions of entrepreneurs and leaders to become more empowered to tackle bigger problems. This book is part of that vision. The ideas in this book are designed for quality businesses that care about what they do and want to be able to take their products to market more effectively. They are not for people who want to run a gimmick, make a fast sale or pull a swift win over their unsuspecting buyers.

Before you even begin, you must feel confident that your offering is something that genuinely serves people. You must be passionate about it and the value it presents to the world. You must love what you do, care about your customers and want to be in your business for the long haul. For the rest of this book, I will assume that's a given.

Being oversubscribed is the way for you to do your best work and spend more time with your current clients rather than chasing new ones. It gives you more downtime to innovate your products rather than running around selling them – and it allows you to build your brand rather than blending in with the crowd.

I've also written this book because I understand the struggle most entrepreneurs and leaders undergo.

We live in remarkable, changing times. Many ideas that worked five years ago aren't working anymore. Everyone is under pressure to innovate and put results on the board. The decade ahead is going to be both challenging and inspiring. The pace of change is speeding up and the way the world of business and society works won't look the same in ten years from now.

Many people will see this as a great wave of change that sweeps them out to sea, while others view it as one they can surf and enjoy. If you're like me, you'll be paddling hard.

By the end of this book, you'll have a method for becoming oversubscribed. I'm going to unpack a process for getting yourself in the enviable position of being in demand. Of course, it will be up to you to apply the process to your business – and it'll take trial and error before you get it right. Ideas are easy; it's the implementation that's hard. Stick with it though, because the payoff is extraordinary. Once you are oversubscribed you'll earn more money, have more fun and attract more opportunities.

You won't have to chase opportunities; you'll curate those that show up. Your inbox will become a garden of prospects rather than an endless stream of tasks to follow up on.

This book isn't just about marketing principles and business methods. I will begin by addressing some problems that most businesses suffer from and sharing some of the stories and principles that drive the deeper philosophy behind the book. My goal is for you to understand these concepts on a deep enough level that you'll make better decisions intuitively and you'll be approaching your business with a different outlook.

You might need to read this book several times and let the ideas sink in for that to happen. Some of the ideas are subtly woven into the stories. There's a rich tapestry out there and you're part of it. But as with any tapestry, you can't see it if you don't have the right perspective. When you take a few steps back you can see the bigger picture.

I'm hoping this book gives you a look at the bigger picture for you and your business. Let's begin a journey together that starts where you are right now and leads you to where you want to be.

PART I

PRINCIPLES FOR BECOMING OVERSUBSCRIBED

PRINCIPLE 1

DEMAND AND SUPPLY SET THE PRICE

You likely learned long ago that the market forces of demand and supply determine the price and the profit you'll make. But what you didn't learn is that you can make your own market forces.

THE STORY OF THE TWO BIDDERS

I was in a room with 400 people who had come to see renowned entrepreneur and author, Gary Vaynerchuk, share his ideas on social media marketing. He announced at the end of his presentation that he'd be auctioning off a 1-hour one-on-one business consultation with him and the proceeds would go to charity.

He explained that the last time he did a consultation like this he had made several introductions to his network and the person had made an additional $50,000 in less than 30 days. "It's not just a consultation", he explained. "It's potentially access to my network – and I know some of the world's most powerful people."

This had put the audience into a state of frenzy. I opened the auction with a bid of £500 and immediately another person took it to £600. Within a flash the price hit £1,000 and the hands kept popping up.

Bids were coming in thick and fast. £2,000, £2,200, £2,400, £2,600, £2,800.

As the bidding passed the £3,000 mark, it came down to two men who clearly both wanted this prize. Everyone else was out of the race, but these two guys kept matching each other and taking the price up another £100 each time.

They were the only two people still bidding in a room with 400 individuals. The rest were sitting patiently or enjoying the spectacle.

The price got up to £3,900 with no signs of slowing down. Gary could tell the audience members were getting restless – so he asked the two bidders, "Will you both pay £4,000 each and I will provide a consultation for both of you?"

They agreed, and the hammer went down. Gary had raised £8,000 by auctioning off two hours of his time.

I'm not sure how high it would have gone but I do know that it only takes two people to push up the price at an auction. Most of the people in the room didn't bid at all and very few people bid beyond £1,500. But that doesn't matter. When the supply is "one" and there are "two" who want it, then that price keeps going up. Two people who desire something is enough to oversubscribe the one person who has it. The price keeps going up until one entity gives in.

When Facebook purchased cross-platform mobile messaging app WhatsApp for $19 billion, the number seemed ridiculous to almost everyone on the planet – except one other bidder. Google was the other company who wanted to buy WhatsApp and the two rival companies bid the price into the stratosphere. Had the price been set by a wider market, the general consensus would have been a much lower number.

Too many business owners focus on the entire market place. They are deeply concerned by what the majority will pay rather than finding the small group of people who really value what they offer. But if you focus on the wider market price, you'll always be average.

If Gary Vaynerchuk wanted to try and sell everyone an hour of his time during the auction, he would have probably needed to lower his prices to £200 per hour. And after delivering a month of solid consultations to all 400 people he also would have needed a holiday – and would have had zero energy to write more books or give more talks.

As it turns out, Gary knew that his real value wasn't even the consultation. It was his ability to make a high level introduction that would be taken seriously because it came from him.

Your value is much higher than you think to a small number of people. You don't need everyone on the planet to see you as in demand; you only need enough people who can drive your price up. Separating from the economy and from your industry requires that you turn your attention to those people who find you highly valuable – and then serve them better than anyone else can.

If two people want your time and only one can get it, your price rises until one of them gives in. Your job isn't to please everyone. Your job is to find those people who can't live without you. So…who are those people? What is it they want? And where *do* you find them? These questions matter more than the questions that relate to the overall market.

Your price isn't fixed, or set by the overall market. It's a result of being oversubscribed or not.

Let's begin with some basics that I was taught by one of the world's top market traders.

SOME PEOPLE MISS OUT

"Why do markets go up?"

I was sitting in the home office of one of Australia's most successful stock market traders – a man who had traded billions of dollars and who'd been consistently successful trading markets for 20+ years. He was a man for whom people travelled internationally to hear him speak about markets for an hour or two.

I was 22 years old at the time, and I answered him with my best guess: "Positive news, a good economy, monetary policy, a good CEO; probably they all have an impact, I think."

"Nice try – but no" he said with a smile, "Markets go up because there are more buyers than sellers…and that's it!"

I had forgotten the fundamental truth of economics: the basics of "demand and supply" that you learn on day one of any economics class. A strong market, a good business plan or a compelling story all help but ultimately your price is set by the balance of supply and demand.

What's more, the market abhors a profit. A profit is only tolerated if demand is higher than supply. No one wants your business to be highly profitable other than its stakeholders. If you tell consumers they can have a cheaper price but the company will lose money and might go out of business, they probably won't even think twice about buying as much as they can. They aren't worried about your profit margins; they are concerned about their own budgets.

This is why you'll only make a profit if you are over-subscribed on your capacity to deliver, and why demand for your stuff must always be greater than your ability to supply it.

People forget the basics. They get caught up in tactics for marketing and lead generation, and they fuss over management styles and team-building techniques, forgetting that all of these activities don't mean much if the business isn't oversubscribed.

The principles set out in this book can be useful across many aspects of your business. For example, if you want to hire top talent, you need to be oversubscribed for top talent. That means that some people need to miss out on the job. If you want impactful publicity you need to be oversubscribed for people who want the story you have to share, so some news outlets won't get the story. If you want to sell products, those products need more buyers than supply can allow for – so again, some people will miss out.

Being oversubscribed requires nothing more than a situation whereby some people who really wanted something had to miss out on having it. Of course, it's a difficult situation because you and your company don't *want* people to miss out. Naturally, you want to sell to everyone who's willing to buy, yet that very mindset prevents you from becoming oversubscribed.

Lots of people want a Ferrari – but the people at Ferrari aren't losing sleep over it. They know that the fact that some people have to miss out is what makes their automobile so coveted. Every product that is oversubscribed has people who didn't get it, even though they were *willing* to buy.

If you can get the balance right and keep yourself over-subscribed – disappointing those people who missed out without them losing interest in you entirely, while still delivering remarkable value to those who got through – you'll have no problems being profitable. If supply is too great and everyone who wants what you have can get what you have, the prices will fall and so will the margins. Eventually your business will make losses.

If you want to be oversubscribed you'll need to get comfortable with some people missing out on what you have to offer. That's how the market works – and that's how it determines your rewards.

PROFITS, LOSSES OR WAGES?

There are three ways the demand and supply equation can play out for your business:

1 **Oversubscribed** – Demand is outstripping supply, resulting in profit being tolerated on top of normal wages.

2 **Balanced** – Demand and Supply are relatively even resulting in normal wages being tolerated but not profit.

3 **Undersubscribed** – Excess supply is available above demand, resulting in losses.

It doesn't matter what the product is. The only thing that matters is the relationship between demand and supply. Even when the product stays the same, if that relationship changes, the profitability changes.

In California in the 1980s, millions of people decided that they wanted plastic surgery. The surgeons who could deliver this service were in short supply and they made vast sums of money providing breast enhancements, nose jobs and Botox. Anyone who could perform these operations ended up with a mansion, a yacht, 10 cars and lucrative investments. They were making millions because the market had vastly more buyers than sellers when it came to plastic surgeons.

This is no longer the case nowadays. LA is filled with plastic surgeons. Attracted by the vast available wealth, a whole lot of medical students switched their major in the late 1980s and headed for Beverly Hills to make big money. But they discovered upon arriving that they weren't the only ones who had this incredible brain wave. By the end of the 90s the demand and supply relationship returned to a balance and today most plastic surgeons in LA make a normal surgeon's wage.

The plastic surgeons made more money because of a boom that happened across their whole industry. But as you'll see later in this book, it's possible to be completely independent of your industry and build a market of your own. Most people focus on the market that they are in when they think about demand and supply, but in doing so they miss out on an important part of the story. There are cycles in the economy whereby demand from "consumers" as a whole outstrips supply from "industry" as a whole. In these times, everyone seems to be doing well and there's an economic boom for almost everyone such as happened in the era known as the Roaring Twenties.

There are also cycles in your industry whereby demand for *anyone* in a chosen field of work will be outstripped by the available supply. This is known as an industry boom; for example, the dot-com boom in the late 90s, whereby almost any Silicon Valley company could raise millions for little more than an idea.

It's also possible for businesses and people who play an advanced game to go another layer deep and separate from both the economy and your industry and become a market on your own. You become subject to your own forces of demand and supply independent of anyone else. This is where you can become oversubscribed on your own terms.

The forces of demand and supply work the same when customers and clients see you as separate from your industry. However, you don't need very many people in order to become oversubscribed and to maintain a profitable price if you can get a few key things right.

SEPARATE YOURSELF FROM *THE* MARKET

How to Create Your Own Market

Let's take a look at actors in the USA as an example of an industry in oversupply. There are over 450,000 people who have a Screen Actors Guild (Screen Actors Guild-American Federation of Television and Radio Artists) membership and there are barely 4,500 actors who make better than minimum wage from their acting income. About 99% of actors can't afford to live on the money they earn from acting. Of the 1% that does earn some money, fewer than 1,000 actors in the USA make over US$150,000 a year.

From an economic standpoint there is a massive over-supply of screen actors. So, there's absolutely no reason why a producer would pay a large sum for an actor. Yet, as we know, they do it all the time. For some actors, a fee of millions per film isn't only a possibility; people line up to pay it. These actors are separate from the market. They have made their own market.

George Clooney, Brad Pitt, Sandra Bullock, Cameron Diaz and Julia Roberts have millions of people who will go and see a film if they are in it. They have created their own market and they are oversubscribed. Their income isn't linked to "the" market; it's linked to *their* market.

Champagne brand, Moët & Chandon, has its own market. The price of other sparkling wine from the region doesn't affect them. Their bottles are always oversubscribed because people want to buy their brand.

Tory Burch handbags and shoes aren't affected by the market price of handbags. Burch made a billion dollars during the great recession while most other brand was on sale.

Her brand is oversubscribed because she's built a special relationship with a new type of buyer.

Berkshire Hathaway shares aren't driven by the normal price of other stocks. They have a dedicated following of people who buy into Warren Buffet's philosophy.

You have likely assumed up to this point that your business must operate at the whims of the market as though your income is impacted by the economy and that your lifestyle is inextricably linked to what happens "out there" in your industry. If you're linking your business to the industry, to the market and to the trends that everyone else is following, then you'll continue competing on price with everyone else.

If you separate from *the* market and build *your own* market, you can generate as much money as your market will allow for.

You start this by building your own group of loyal fans. Cultivate a tribe of people who are loyal to your business, your products, your personality and your philosophy. Rally your own troops. Break those people away from the industry, separate them one by one from the market and make them part of something special.

We're going to explore several ways to carve out your own market.

You'll also discover that you don't need to create a massive market for yourself in order to be oversubscribed. As I illustrated earlier, two bidders who really want something can be enough to make the price rise. A small lifestyle business may only need a few thousand loyal customers – and an international business can thrive with a relatively small, dedicated fan-base of people who really love what you do.

YOU DON'T NEED EVERYONE

Jean-Pierre De Villiers (or JP as he's known) is one of London's most highly-paid fitness trainers. However, you have probably never heard of him – because he only has eight key clients!

JP's clients pay him up to £40,000 per year. They pay six months of their fees in advance and they keep renewing with him. If you call JP and ask to become a client, he will ask you a few questions and based on how you answer he will either recommend another trainer or he will tell you that he might be able to work with you in 6–12 months.

JP only works with high-flying wealthy men who travel all the time, earn over £400,000 per year, and who believe in his personal fitness philosophy. He doesn't need everyone to be a client; he needs eight people who want a dedicated level of service that most trainers are too busy to deliver.

Of course, he didn't begin his career this way. When I first met JP in 2010, his fee was £45 per hour. He was burned out working from 6 a.m. to 8 p.m., six days a week. If you called him back, then he would tell you that he would find a way to squeeze you in even if it meant he started earlier or finished later. He was very accommodating to new clients.

I met JP when he was at breaking point. If it wasn't for the fact he's both physically and mentally strong he could have burned himself out much sooner. We talked about the concept that he could be high value for a small number of people and that we should try to find this market.

He resisted me at first and said that there was a "market rate" for fitness trainers in London and that £40–£60 an hour was the going rate. I smiled and asked him to trust me.

JP worked hard to identify his niche; he wrote a book, tailored his offering to his market and raised his profile. He spoke at business events and was featured in exclusive magazines. He positioned himself as a Key Person of Influence in the eyes of an elite target audience. All of this new activity began to build a new market around him, a market that wasn't the "London fitness market". It was the "JP market".

Within the circle of people he attracted were a small number of men who fit his new criteria. The wanted someone like JP who could get them fit despite their gruelling schedule and their strong personalities.

For all the other people that JP attracted, he launched 10-day fitness retreats in Thailand. Twice a year he takes a group of 20 people out to the tropical beaches of Thailand where they practise intensive martial arts fitness. His retreats are as oversubscribed as his training sessions are.

In 2013, most people didn't buy the alternative digital currency known as "Bitcoin". In fact, most people hadn't even heard of a Bitcoin. The idea of a digital currency that was somehow pegged to a mathematical equation was surely some sort of joke.

However, it really didn't matter what "most people" thought. A small number of people saw the potential of "crypto-currency" and they bid the price through the roof. The price went from $20 to $1,000 per Bitcoin in 12 months, as more and more people "got it". The traditional markets didn't understand it and it really didn't matter. At that time, demand was greater than supply and Bitcoins were oversubscribed so the price kept going up.

You will suffer if you try to cater to what the market thinks. The market will force your prices down and demand more and more from you until you snap. Rather than catering to the market, let's get better at finding *your* market. And *your* market is made up of the people who really care about what you do. They place a high value on the results you can bring them. They "get it", and importantly, they can also afford it. You know these people better than they know themselves when it comes to being able to surprise and delight them. You understand their unmet needs and wants; you have insights for them that will blow them away. You care about these people almost to a fault.

These are the people into whom you put your energy. Over time you'll separate your market from everyone else and they will be immune to some cheap offer or cheesy ploy offered by a competitor; if it's not from you, they won't respond. You don't need everyone in order to become over-subscribed, you only need more people than you can handle.

FAMOUS FOR A FEW

In some ways, I suppose I'm like a celebrity. I get interviewed on podcasts; people watch my videos, read my books and attend my events. But the difference between me and "other celebrities" is that I'm famous for a small number of people – thousands rather than millions.

The good news is that's all it takes these days. You don't need to be on the big screen, talked about on gossip blogs or forever on the front page of the paper in order to have a fantastic business or life. You just need to be famous for a few thousand people.

But what does "famous" mean?

It means that someone has never met you but they feel like they know, like and trust you. They'd recognize you if they did meet you and they'd be pleased to see you. They've read several of your articles, watched a dozen of your online videos, bought your products and follow what you do.

If you can get 5,000–10,000 people who are in that camp, you'll have a wonderful, oversubscribed small business. You'll also get ongoing speaking opportunities, requests to consult on projects, invitations to comment in industry publications – and your "fame" will be sustainable. You'll feel accomplished and enjoy life.

What's more, if you're smart about it, you'll be able to do this from anywhere in the world and have a coveted "lifestyle business".

If you're running a corporate business, the numbers might be 100,000+ to one million people, but the principle is the same; you don't need everyone to know about you. You want a core group of people who really care about what you're up to.

So what are the key ingredients for being "famous"?

1 **Consistent and repetitive message** – This means you need to repeatedly state what you do in very clear and

credible terms. Don't radically change it each time or for each audience. People need to hear something about 7–15 times before they "get it" and remember it. If you're going to have 5,000 people "get it" you need to arrive at one way of "showing up" or describing what you do and then say it a lot.

2 **Content** – People read all the time. They Google stuff, they share stuff, they read what their friends are reading, they email links to a friend; then on holiday they take a Kindle and read some more! If you haven't got articles, blogs, books, reports, videos, podcasts or updates for people to read, then it's nearly impossible to become famous for even 500 people.

3 **Commercial ecosystem** – After people get to know you, like you and trust you, they want to buy from you. Some will want to buy something small for £100; some will want to buy something for £1,000 and a small number of people will want to spend much more than that with you. This means you need a product ecosystem for people to engage with.

4 **Continuity** – When people "discover you", they want to know what went on before. So they Google you, look around, piece together your timeline. This means you need to have an online profile that shows what you've been doing over the last few years. Then they want to stay updated with what you're doing in the future. People will want to follow you on Twitter, Facebook, YouTube and the like.

5 **Collaboration** – As you become famous to 5,000+ people, you'll get opportunities to do deals with other people who are famous to a similar group. They might want to create a product together, promote an event or work on a project. You'll need a good framework for what you say yes to and what you turn down.

People used to strive for their "15 minutes of fame"; however, that type of success is pretty fruitless. It's far better to become famous for 5,000 people and stay that way. You won't be able to set up your mansion in Beverly Hills but you'll enjoy a very fun lifestyle and reap all sorts of benefits. Who knows? You might even get stopped on the street once in a while.

THE FOUR DRIVERS FOR A MARKET IMBALANCE: INNOVATION, RELATIONSHIPS, CONVENIENCE AND PRICE

We already discussed that the way to being oversubscribed is to achieve an imbalance where there are more buyers than sellers. There are four drivers of market imbalances where you'll see more buyers than sellers. These are the four ways to achieve this imbalance.

1 **Innovation** – You create something new and shiny, that no one else sells. There's only one seller (you) and a niche of new buyers who want it. There are therefore more

buyers than sellers by virtue of the fact there's only one supplier and more people who want it.

2 **Relationships** – You build such a powerful relationship with buyers that they ignore other sellers. There are more buyers than sellers because buyers aren't interested in other sellers.

3 **Convenience** – You are answering the needs of the market with the most frictionless expression of what they want. This is about being in the right place, at the right time, with something that meets consumers' unmet desires. This creates more buyers than sellers because buyers are reluctant to invest time, money and energy finding alternatives.

4 **Price** – This occurs when you're able to create an imbalance based on price. You've invested into an asset that creates an efficiency others don't have. Crucially, you're still able to offer your products at a price that is profitable but that price is lower than other suppliers can achieve.

If you look carefully at large and established markets you'll see that there are often four big players who each occupy one of these market positions. You can see it in hotels, airlines, banks, telecommunications, cars and computers. Essentially, the big brands focus on dominating one of these four market imbalances and choose one of the others as a secondary.

You'll also notice that each one of these positions has an opposite. You can't be highly innovative and convenient; it doesn't work because innovation takes time to scale. You can't be super cheap and also compete on relationships; it costs money to build relationships. So you'll have to choose one main market position for your business to focus on.

Let's look at each one in more detail to help you determine which will work best for you.

Driver # 1 – Innovation

The first way to create more buyers than sellers is to create something new that the market hasn't seen before and they now want. An iPod in 2002, a Furby in 1999, a geometric perm in 1963. On a local level it could be a new style of Reiki massage, the only organic cafe in the area, a new website traffic strategy.

Have you ever noticed that the top movie of the week is always a new movie? It never goes backwards to *Titanic* or *The Godfather*. Even if it isn't anywhere near as good as some of the classics, people love experiencing new things. The new and shiny thing you create doesn't need to be an epic blockbuster and it doesn't need to be for the mass market.

An innovation can be subtle. It can be the way you package something up with other products and services. It can be something new you've brought in from a different market. It can be something people have seen before but with a new feature.

Judy Craymer, the founder of Littlestar Services, had a love for ABBA music. She decided to turn their music into the stage show *Mamma Mia!* The "repackaging" earned her company over $2.5 billion in sales revenue. It was a subtle innovation that was powerful enough to capture a lot of attention.

My team and I created the "Key Person of Influence" programme in 2010. It's a fresh look at leadership and entrepreneurship combining elements from a Silicon Valley growth accelerator with training and development programmes. That innovation has become a global business serving thousands of entrepreneurs and leaders from several countries.

There are three main types of innovation:

Product innovation: You invest in a new product that people haven't seen before, or modify an existing product in a new way. For example, George Lucas invented a galaxy of characters and products when he unleashed *Star Wars* on the world.

Systems innovation: You deliver an existing product in a new way that makes things faster or more reliable. For example, Facebook is an innovative system for people to keep track of all their friends and it's a great system for advertisers too.

Brand innovation: You make something boring a lot more desirable with a new way of packaging it for the market. For example, Ralph Lauren popularized the standard polo shirt through high fashion branding.

DRIVER # 2 - RELATIONSHIP

The second way to ensure you have more buyers than sellers is to own the relationship with the buyers in your market so that they become more loyal or they don't shop around so much. Have you ever stopped to think whom you might use as an alternative to your accountant? Is your accountant even number one? Does he/she charge a lot more than others, is he/she about the same as others – or is he/she a lot cheaper?

If you haven't really considered these questions before – and most people haven't – it is because your accountant owns the relationship with you and you have stopped shopping around. If your accountant can build up more and more clients like you over time, they will earn a very good income from their practice.

Another way to achieve this is through contracts. I remember when I was looking around for phone plans. I must have wasted 50 hours of my life trying to understand the difference between "Go Time", "Stop the Clock" and "Mega Minutes". While I was desperately trying to work out which plan would be best for me, there were options appearing everywhere. Ads, brochures, offers and signs were jumping out at me all the time with different ways to "save money" on my phone bill.

After a while I realized that they were all pretty much the same and that my time was probably better spent on other things, so I signed a 24-month contract with a carrier. Something strange happened the very next day – no more ads. They vanished from my existence because my new carrier owned the relationship with me and I stopped looking around.

There is another way to own a relationship with the market. You can become an influencer in your field so that people will listen to your advice rather than shop around.

This is the reason that Roger Federer gets paid millions to endorse tennis products and why restaurants bend over backwards for food critics, or mutual funds court the favour of financial advisors. All of these people have their market listening to their advice.

Why would I shop around for tennis gear when I know what racket Roger Federer uses? Why would I try all the restaurants in London when I could just go to the one that was rated five stars by the local food critic? Why try to understand financial markets when my trusted financial planner has all the answers?

Owning the relationship is a powerful way to become oversubscribed – and there are three ways to do this:

1 **Become more influential:** Improve your ability to enroll others in your ideas and projects.

2 **Become better known:** Widen your own personal or your business's appeal through media, events, publicity and other brand-building activities.

3 **Get deals in place:** Once a deal is done, customers stop shopping around. Creating lasting agreements with clients gives your business more strength and value.

DRIVER # 3 - CONVENIENCE

Market "friction" refers to the time, energy, effort and know-how required to buy something. If it's difficult to buy something because it's far away, poorly understood or time consuming, the market is slowing down due to friction.

If you can reduce that friction, you'll attract a lot of customers – who will call it a convenience.

When you find ways to simplify and speed up the process of buying from you, it creates a market imbalance. People buy from you because it's much easier than going elsewhere. Over the last 15 years we've seen many successful businesses build up because they took a traditional business into the digital world. They reduced friction or, put another way, increased convenience.

Amazon almost dealt a death blow to traditional bookstores because it made it a lot easier to buy a book. Each book is exactly the same if you buy it in a store or online but the ease and simplicity of Amazon makes them the default option.

Another outcome of convenience is often called a trend. Before a trend starts, many people are already buying something but it's happening slowly because it's difficult to buy or it's difficult to get information. It's inconvenient for most buyers. The trend often kicks off when information becomes more widely available or distribution issues are solved.

However, it's worth remembering that trends these days come and go very quickly. Items will trend for a little while but thanks to the Internet, anything that's trending is quickly accounted for with other sellers. The barriers to entry for convenience are lower than ever.

Convenience or less friction occurs in three ways:

1 **Better distribution:** When a business makes something available to its buyers with less energy, effort or time required.
2 **Better market information:** As more information is made available, market leaders give way to market followers. This also occurs when a buyer doesn't need to research their options as much.
3 **Automation:** When things happen faster or on autopilot. This could be new machinery or systems online or offline.

DRIVER # 4 - PRICE

The final way to create more buyers than sellers is to bring down the cost of production so that you can offer something cheaper than everyone else but still make a profit.

Many small services businesses compete on price because they don't have the high overheads that large companies do. They can run their business from the spare room, piggyback on market trends, use cheap software, keep costs low – and still earn a better income than if they were sat at an expensive desk in the city with an expensive brand behind them.

Big businesses used to be able to dominate low prices because they could afford to invest in plant and equipment that would create a barrier to entry. But thanks to today's "collaborative economy" most of the plant and equipment is available to smaller businesses when they need it and it's not their problem when they don't.

There are of course some investments that still create barriers to entry and allow prices to stay low. When Andrew Lloyd Webber came up with several hit stage shows he made a lot of money, which he then used to buy up the major theatres in London. Because he owns the property, he doesn't have to write shows nowadays; if you want to get your play to run in London you will have to use his property. He can also afford to run his own plays at a lower cost because he owns the venues.

There are three ways you can reduce costs and still keep your margins:

1 **Invest:** Cleverly investing into assets that create a natural barrier to entry will allow you to reduce your costs and keep your margins. Owning your premises or buying

equipment that is expensive to hire can be ways to keep prices lower.

2 **Refine:** Looking for inefficiencies where there are costs that do not increase the value to a paying customer will keep margins wide while prices fall.

3 **Systemize:** Using systems and technology rather than people is a powerful way to keep overheads low and margins high.

BUYING ENVIRONMENTS CREATE BUYERS

People don't buy for logic or reason; they buy because the conditions are right. Buying behaviour is stimulated by the buying environment.

I did an event in Australia where I gave a two-day masterclass on the topic of creating "Campaign Driven Enterprises". Rather than releasing the tickets, I advised the promotional team running the event to use one of the principles we teach at that workshop called "transparency of movement". It works like this: we sent out a Facebook post asking a group of people if they would be interested in attending the workshop at a price of $795. We explained that the workshop was only for 60 people in both locations because it was designed to be highly interactive. We advised that we would only consider running the workshop if there was at least 50 people interested in each location.

Within 48 hours, over 175 people had posted on the Facebook thread that they were interested and willing to pay the price. Additionally, many of the people started asking if they could bring their marketing team along too.

We then told the group that we would release the tickets the following day at 9 a.m. and there would only be 120 tickets in total, including the additional team members people wanted to bring. By the end of the first day, almost all of the tickets had sold out and had been paid in full. Before I had even booked my flights, we had almost $100,000 in the bank account. It was less than 10 days from the moment we discussed the idea to the time the money had cleared in the bank. The workshops were sold out four months in advance.

The reason this worked so well was because of the transparency of movement. People could see that there were over 175 people who had posted in the Facebook thread. If they looked closely, they could see that many people actually wanted to bring several guests along with them. These workshops were clearly oversubscribed. By giving genuine reasons why we could only have a total of 120 people attend these workshops, we provided a clear incentive to sign up quickly once tickets became available.

Conversely, had the team called through the exact same database of people and tried to sell tickets one at a time, I don't believe they could have filled the workshops in a month, let alone 10 days. People likely would have opted to sign up closer to the date or said, "call me back when it starts to fill up". The energy would have been lost, the momentum wouldn't have gained traction – and the team would have had to work a lot harder to get the same result.

The herd moves when the herd moves. Trying to get one member of the pack to run forward is hard unless they are part of a stampede. Your goal as a "Campaign Driven Enterprise" isn't to engage people one at a time – it's to cause a mad dash all at once.

PEOPLE DON'T BUY WHAT OTHERS WANT TO SELL. THEY BUY WHAT OTHERS WANT TO *BUY*.

Paris department store Galeries Lafayette is one of the world's most famous places to buy high-end fashion and accessories. Inside is an exclusive area that stocks Chanel handbags, but customers cannot enter just by walking in; they have to line up at the entrance. Then an attendant comes by and asks what you'll be looking at in the store. The wait isn't normally too long – only about 10 minutes or so, and the attendants are quite pleasant. Then you're in the store and you're pleased to be able to finally browse a very limited range of designer handbags.

You look around, spot something you like, and feel incredibly lucky to be able to finally hold it. You don't take too long, people are lining up behind you and they can't come into the store until you've finished. You make your selection and snap up one of the bags at a price that could buy a full set of luggage (and probably the airfare to wherever you're going as well). The store's attendants thank you and you leave proudly as you bask in the adoration of the people who await the same opportunity.

Outside only three streets away is a store full to the brim with handbags, belts, shoes and jewelry. A man stands on the street shouting partly in French and partly in English about how his stock is on sale, it's cheap, it's half-priced. People try to ignore him; they make an arc around the store pretending not to notice him in his desperation. They glance inside and they notice the store is mostly empty other than a few older tourists who are hopefully too deaf to be put off by the shouting.

The handbags in both these stores aren't that different. Clearly the genuine Chanel bags would cost a little bit more to make and would last a little bit longer; but if aliens landed on Earth and had to figure out which one was better, they might struggle with the challenge.

There is, of course, one big difference – the prices. The brand name bags cost fifty times more than the street store bags. Yet that's the one people queue up for, while the one that's barely selling for its production costs isn't getting anyone engaged.

The reason is because people don't buy what others want to sell; they buy what other people want to buy. We buy properties and clothes that other people want; we buy from consulting firms that others use; and we invest in companies that other investors are throwing money at. Yet countless companies make the mistake of going to great lengths to show how badly they want to sell something. They set up stores everywhere; they mark their prices down; they scream into the streets that they have "cheap" products to sell.

Service providers take on clients without setting any boundaries. They answer calls late at night, get paid late and incur costs. Everything about the typical service provider screams, "I will do anything for a sale".

But the more companies do that, the more they turn people off. The more a potential buyer sees you are desperate to sell something the more they wonder why you're so desperate.

Your goal is place a high value on what you do and work with people who do as well. Set your boundaries, have your terms, protect your space so you can deliver something special.

The skill comes in making something available without forcing it on people. Your job is to celebrate the people who are already buying from you and to hold them in the highest esteem. Rather than completing a transaction and then looking for the next buyer, take more time to care for the person who just bought from you. Take the time to make sure they feel good about their purchase and they are given more than they expected. Don't rush off; build the relationship.

When people feel good about buying from you, they will tell people that they bought from you. When they tell people they bought from you, other people will want to buy from you too. When people want to buy from you, you're on your way to being oversubscribed.

TURN YOUR CLIENTS INTO CELEBRITIES

The DJ is playing a sublime set of new music, the sun is going down over the water, beautiful people are dancing, fresh sushi is being served and there's a lineup out the front of Nikki Beach Nightclub in Majorca. Despite the fact you're paying a fortune, you feel lucky to be part of this electric atmosphere. For a brief moment of time, you kid yourself that you're a bit like a celebrity as you soak it all in.

Through the crowd of people, six gorgeous staff members make their way across the dance floor. They have in their hands a gigantic, silver ice bucket with a bottle of champagne in it. Blazing alongside the bubbly, giant sparklers shower the dance floor with a mini-fireworks display.

The bottle arrives at the table, the cork is popped, the sparklers continue to fizz and the DJ gives your group a little wave as we all clink glasses. This might be the stupidest

£300 you've ever spent – but you're all feeling pretty thrilled, and everyone in the club now wants a bottle of champagne too.

This club understands what it means to celebrate your customers. They don't need to try and sell champagne with pushy sales people; instead, they have turned their clients into celebrities and made their product something to aspire to.

Most businesses don't do this. They are overly focused on people who haven't yet bought from them. They constantly think about the non-buyers. They chase them and spend a fortune on trying to coerce them to part with their cash. Yet the moment that someone does finally buy, they are rapidly forgotten. "We have your cash – now on to the next sale" seems to be most businesses' mantra these days.

But oversubscribed businesses don't think like that. They understand that if you treat your clients as aspirational individuals, many more people will aspire to be like them too.

Celebrate your clients. Make them the stars of your show. Get famous on their success stories. Take all that money you want to spend on getting a new client and spend it on celebrating your existing clients. Put them high on a pedestal for everyone to see.

We built our business by sharing client success stories. As soon as people started hearing our client case studies, we had people beating down the door to be the next one. We put our clients on stage at our events; we filmed them telling their story; we put those videos on our YouTube channel and we created printed materials that talked about their businesses, not ours. We used our marketing budget to throw exclusive events for our existing clients; new potential clients couldn't come.

Rather than beating your drum about yourself, beat the drum for your clients. Help them create a huge success story and then showcase it. Treat your clients like celebrities and let them pull a crowd. In most industries, if you genuinely do focus on the success of your clients you will stand out like a beacon and become massively oversubscribed as a byproduct.

PEOPLE DON'T BUY WHAT THEY NEED – THEY BUY WHAT THEY WANT

Singapore has one of the highest-density populations on earth and its government doesn't like cars very much. As such, they charge an insanely high tax on vehicles to discourage people from buying them. A basic car in Singapore costs more than a luxury car in the UK or USA. There are no long stretches of winding, scenic roads in Singapore and the top speed limit is only 90km per hour.

Despite all of these facts, Singapore sells more Ferraris per person than almost any other country.

No one in Singapore *needs* a Ferrari. It is, in fact, a ridiculous car to own in this particular country. There's not a single place on the island that a Ferrari would be fun to drive; it's nearly impossible to get a super-car past second gear in Singapore. So considering that Singapore is also one of the most expensive places to buy a Ferrari (about 4x more than in the UK) why do so many people have them?

They buy them because *they want one.*

People don't buy what they need or what they should buy; they buy what they want.

Singaporeans who have made a lot of money want a Ferrari – and that's all that matters. It doesn't matter how poorly suited this car is, how expensive it is, or how much more comfortable they would be in a sedan. What they need doesn't matter; what they *want* reigns supreme.

You can go broke trying to tell people what they need. However, you will do very well if you figure out what people want and figure out how to get it for them. Need is logical and want is emotional. Emotions will win every time, even with the most intelligent people.

People don't need a $500 Mont Blanc Pen, an expensive Rolex watch, to buy a rental property in London, or to spend extra money for lululemon yoga pants, but they want them.

Therefore, if you present your business, your products or your ideas as something that people need or should have, you're running an awfully big risk. Regardless of how right you may be, you might not get the customer. Think about it: no one had to run a marketing campaign for people to get rid of their VHS and start buying DVDs. We just wanted better quality movies.

I know a health business that made the mistake of trying to explain to people what they need to do. Even when people agreed with them, they simply didn't buy. Instead they bought the pill, the liposuction, the gimmicky equipment. That same business took off when it started to talk to people about what they *wanted*. The language changed, the conversation changed and the energy towards buying something changed too. What didn't change was the *actual product itself.* The same health club membership, food plan and positive habits still comprised the offer but – because they were packaged in alignment to a want rather than a need, they started to sell.

Social change works the same way. Experts agree the world probably needs to adopt a vegetarian diet, but it doesn't really want to. Until a company makes us hunger to eat less meat, we won't stop. The world needs to get food to a billion people, but it doesn't really want to. Only when people thirst to make this a reality will it happen. The world needs to stop putting Photoshopped, size zero supermodels on billboards and magazines, but it doesn't really want to. When we feel attracted to a more realistic image of beauty, fashion retailers will change. The world needs to stop producing so much plastic, but it doesn't really want to. When we begin to put recyclable goods in the trolley for the love of it, we will see less plastic.

All of these things won't happen unless people *want to do them*, no matter how much we might need to. Organizations that try to tell us what we need to do will ultimately fail; organizations that make social change desirable, interesting, cool and fun will win. Charity: Water was launched in 2006 by an ex-nightclub promoter, Scott Harrison, who understood the power of branding and celebrity endorsement. He created an ultra-cool campaign around the concept of donating your birthday. Participants raise money for clean water in Africa by requesting a donation rather than a gift and this simple idea is raising over $20m a year to fulfil an important mission.

Whether you're focused on running a business or creating a social movement, the key to your success is tapping into people's wants rather than their needs. Ask people what they want; build it for them the way they want it. Explain it to them in the context of what they want. Then package up what they need along with it.

IT'S OK TO BE DIFFERENT

If you do what others do, you'll get what others get.

THE POWER OF PHILOSOPHY

Pete Evans is a celebrity chef in Australia watched by 4 million people every night. He has a philosophy about food. He believes that food should be healthy and delicious, and that our modern processed diet doesn't work because our bodies have evolved without those things. He believes everyone has a "cooking comfort zone" and it's worth getting out of it and preparing things you've never tried before.

Pete operates according a certain philosophy about food and as a result he polarizes people. Some people agree with his philosophy and become loyal fans, while others think he's too extreme and they push against him. The truer he remains to his philosophy, the more fans he attracts – and the more detractors he deals with.

Occasionally Pete and I discuss how he will comment in the media and the answer always comes back to his philosophy. The more he talks about his beliefs on food in an accessible way, the more people become his loyal fans. Rather than focusing on the people who don't like his philosophy, he focuses on those who do. He creates recipes for them, writes books for them, finds products for them and has conversations online with them.

There's nothing to be gained by being boring, plain and beige, and trying to please everyone. For one thing, it's impossible – and for another, attempting to fit in with the crowd will get you nothing more than the crowd. And you know by now that the goal is to create *your own* crowd and to share your philosophy with them.

Your philosophy is made up of your strongly held beliefs and opinions. It's your take on life and it doesn't need to appeal to everyone.

Environmental activist, Captain Paul Watson, has a philosophy that the environment needs to be protected with brute force. He's willing to go to the icy waters in the southern oceans and put himself and the crew of the Sea Shepherd between a whaling ship and a humpback whale. Not everyone believes in his approach, but enough people do for him to maintain his rebel fleet of ships.

In Bali, there's a retreat for people who believe that fasting and juicing in tropical paradise is a better way to heal

their diseases than spending time in hospital on pharma-ceutical drugs. Some people think these people are crazy or idealistic and are risking their lives. It really doesn't matter what those people think, though, since the retreat is booked for months in advance.

This book contains elements of my philosophy. I'm sure not everyone agrees with my way of approaching the world and I don't need everyone to agree. I'm interested in putting ideas into the world and seeing who shows up as a result.

Facebook founder Mark Zuckerberg has a philosophy that the world should be more open and connected. He also believes privacy is dead. He wants to connect the whole world and that philosophy drives his decisions at Facebook. A lot of people don't agree with the philosophy but he's not doing too badly. Another Facebook persona, Chief

Operations Officer Sheryl Sandberg, has a philosophy that women should "lean in" to their careers. She challenges women to be more ambitious and proactive in the workplace. She released a book touting this philosophy that a lot of people loved it – and also received criticism from people who didn't agree with it. But what matters most is she has millions of people who know what she's about. Those who show up for her are going to be loyal advocates.

Warren Buffet has a philosophy when it comes to investing. Oprah Winfrey has a philosophy on television content. Richard Branson has a philosophy when it comes to building his team and his brand. Technology billionaire, Elon Musk, has a philosophy about why it's important to go to other planets!

When you develop a clear philosophy and you put it out to the world you'll begin to create your own market. Not everyone will agree with you, of course, but if 1,000 people feel strongly about it, you'll have 1,000 people who are your market. If you have no philosophy you appear to be bland and like every other commodity in your market. You're back to competing on price.

What's your philosophy? What are your strongly held beliefs about what you do? What do you stand for? What do you stand *against*? What is the change you want to see in the world?

The clearer you are when answering these questions, the closer you will be to being oversubscribed.

IT'S OK TO FAIL

"Fail whale!" I grumbled. I had composed a tweet and had clicked "send" but instead of seeing my tweet go whizzing around the world to be retweeted, the damn picture of a whale and birds appeared along with the message: "We're unable to cope with current demand."

I'm sure I wasn't the only one to wonder why this basic messaging system was always breaking down in 2009. Considering that Facebook was coping just fine with messages, images, videos, events and likes at that time – and all Twitter had to do was capture 140 characters and send it out to the world – I often wondered, how hard could it be?

Did the "fail whale" make me want to use them less though? Strangely not. Instead it gave Twitter a mystique, signalling to the market that the platform was in such high demand that it almost couldn't handle everyone who wanted to use it. In short, Twitter was oversubscribed.

There's something very powerful about being "unable to cope with demand", yet most people and companies try to hide it. Rather than pretending you're superhuman when you get too busy, tell people that you're currently fully booked and physically unable to cope with the demand. Be polite, be cheerful but be honest about it.

Expose this fact to your clients. Tell them that you'd love to work with them but right now there's not enough room in your office to hire more staff, or you keep running out of the supplies you need. Tell people there's a problem caused by too much demand. Let them know you are working on having it fixed as soon as you can and they should try again soon.

You'll be surprised at the response this generates. Yes, people will be frustrated and annoyed that you're not able to take their business, but they'll be curious and intrigued by it too.

I once called a business coach who was referred to me with a high recommendation by a friend. I left several messages and got a call back a week later. He told me that he was taking six weeks' holiday because he was feeling burned out and that I would have to call him back then.

At first, I thought all the same things you're probably thinking: "What kind of professional coach gets burned out? Shouldn't he have systems and processes that run the business like clockwork?"

Strangely though, I set a reminder in my diary to call him and we had a great first meeting. He was refreshed after his holiday and explained that he had "fired" three clients who he wasn't excited to work with anymore. He then proceeded to interview me as a potential client and give me his list of rules for working with him. He also gave me his holiday times a year in advance and instructed me not to call him during those times. It wasn't a gimmick; he genuinely seemed unfazed by the idea of walking away from my money.

I was shocked – but I also respected it, and I signed on for a $30,000 coaching programme for myself and the team.

It sounds so counter-intuitive – we've all been told that the customer is king. Oversubscribed businesses don't see it that way though. They believe they have something of high value and they can only deliver it properly on certain terms that work for both parties.

They also believe that there are plenty of other people out there who want value and they would rather find someone who agrees to their terms than bend themselves out of shape to meet the demands of others.

Where are the bottlenecks in your business? Is it the delivery systems? The number of senior staff? Your own creativity?

On your journey towards being oversubscribed, it might be wise to be more open about your shortcomings and tactfully enforce measures to ensure you don't break at the seams by overselling your capacity.

IT'S OK TO SAY "NO"

The most famous nightclub in the world during the 1970s was Manhattan's Studio 54. The owners decided early on that they would rather be empty than have the wrong people in the club. They were the first club that famously turned people away for wearing the wrong shoes or not being glamorous enough.

You need to treat your business the same way – as an exclusive club. And just like Studio 54, you must be willing to turn away people at the door if they aren't a good fit.

"No" is powerful. It's a word that is said by people and businesses that are sure of what they do and who they are for.

Only the best restaurants will say no to a reservation. Only the best business consultants will say no to a potential client. Only the best hotels will say no to a booking. Only the best nightclubs will turn someone away at the door. Only the best retail stores will tell someone "No, that jacket doesn't suit you".

Only the best will say no to a person who wants a discount or to bend your rules. Only the best will say no to a talented applicant member who is *almost* but not 100% right for the job. Only the best will say no to a supplier who ticks *most* but not all of the boxes. Only the best will turn down money from an investor when it just doesn't "feel" right, despite the amount of money they're willing to provide.

Google has over one million applicants who apply for just a few thousand jobs each year. They have tests, games, questionnaires and assignments that whittle the numbers down in what appears to be an intellectual's version of *The Hunger Games*. Only the very best can survive and 99% are given a polite "no". At the very end, the most senior executives must sign off on each and every Google employee; often founder Larry Page himself signs off on new hires. Google understands the power of "no"; they are aware that their future depends on being fussy.

Netflix has a policy that states that employees who don't like working for them can get paid $2,000 to quit. They encourage any staff members who aren't happy to put an end to it fast and admit they aren't happy there rather than dragging the process out and bringing bad energy into the team.

Businesses who become oversubscribed know what they want and have no problem saying no to the rest. They know who their best customers are, who their most loyal and productive staff are, the suppliers they want to use and the investors who will work. They say no to anyone and anything that isn't right.

"No" requires you to develop high standards and stick to them.

In my business we interview people before they become clients. And we turn people away all the time that aren't a good fit. We know that we have to spend time and energy on every client. We also know that some people or businesses would be either too much hard work or we would struggle to deliver to them a remarkable result. If someone isn't a good fit with our business, we politely tell them so.

Saying "no" is also about evolving and living up to your philosophy.

Furniture retailer, Ikea, has recently decided it is saying no to doing business in a way that isn't sustainable. Leading companies are saying no to suppliers who don't care about the environment. Many forward-thinking restaurants in

Asia are saying "No, we don't serve shark fin soup here" after it was discovered that 90% of the oceans' sharks have been decimated for this broth.

It might cost you something to say "no" in the short term, but being fussy makes you better and stronger in the long term.

You already have built-in radar that tells you when to say "no". The problems come when you ignore it. Even when your head says "don't take on this client, they will be a complete pain in the ass" you still take them on because they help you pay the bills.

That's not how an oversubscribed business works. An oversubscribed business tunes in to that little voice and acts upon it. An oversubscribed business says, "I think you'd be happier going elsewhere" and doesn't look back. They know that saying no to someone who's not right for the business creates the space for perfect clients to show up.

IT'S OK TO MAKE PEOPLE WAIT

Steve Jobs had only been on stage for a few minutes, but the audience's excitement was already at fever pitch. People had known for weeks that an announcement about a new product was coming, but no one knew what it was going to be. Rumours circulated during the two-day conference, yet no one really was any closer to the facts.

When Jobs walked onto the stage he was relaxed and poised, as he said, "This is a day I've been looking forward to for two and a half years." He began to drop clues: "We're releasing three revolutionary products – a wide screen iPod with touch controls, a revolutionary mobile phone, a breakthrough Internet communications device". Jobs continued to flick through images and while it didn't quite make sense, something appeared all of a sudden. "These are not three separate devices, this is one device. We are calling it an iPhone!"

What happened in the following weeks after the 2007 launch was astounding. People went online and pre-ordered this device by the millions; they lined up outside the retail stores; they badgered their phone companies to break their existing phone contract; and they gladly paid whatever money they had to buy a phone *they had never actually seen.*

From the moment of its first release, the iPhone has become one of the hottest products ever invented. It was launched just before the global recession at a premium price and yet it sold out in days and continued to sell out as fast as they could build them.

It wasn't the first or only smart phone; in fact, there were – and still are – very good alternatives. Yet for the first five years, it outsold the rest of the smart phone market combined.

Was this because the product was genuinely so much better? Was it because retail experience was 10 times better, the processor remarkably faster and people couldn't find anything else that was close? Few people honestly believe that. The real story is about how Steve Jobs got you to want his product, how he made it exclusive and still sold millions of units, how he had people lining up at the stores and how he made people feel they were part of something just by owning this little device.

The real story isn't just the about the gadget itself. It is about the powerful way that great product was brought to market. A large part of this power came because Steve Jobs thought it was OK to make people wait. He made people wait for information, the release date – even outside the physical store before they could buy it.

He made an innovative and high quality product and he emphasized that it would be ready for market on his terms and not beforehand.

Making people wait isn't a bad thing: it allows the hunger to build – sometimes quite literally.

There's a restaurant called Granger & Co in London's exclusive Notting Hill neighbourhood that makes a phenomenally good breakfast. On almost every day of the week, you'll see people lining up out the front (sometimes in the rain), waiting for a table to become available.

What's interesting about this restaurant is that nothing is rushed once you are inside; everything happens at a relaxed pace. It's full but not overcrowded. Staff members seat you, give you menus, come back with your coffee – and give you as much time as you need to make a decision about the food.

They never rush you to finish and free up the table; you can sit and talk for hours if you want. The food is made slowly with fresh ingredients and presented perfectly every time. I presume they don't try and rush the chefs in the kitchen to make it faster. They seem perfectly OK to let people wait outside while they deliver their magic inside.

If Granger & Co crammed the restaurant full of tables, rushed the food preparation and pressured customers to leave quickly, the magic would be lost. There wouldn't be anyone lining up out the front, and there probably wouldn't be anyone inside either.

This business is aware that doing things right takes time. You should never sacrifice your standards in order to squeeze another customer through the door. Making people wait sends a message that what you have is worth waiting for.

Businesses that struggle don't make people wait for quality. Instead, they try every trick in the book to squeeze people in at the expense of the brand experience. They take on customers when they can't deliver, rush the delivery, throw the magic out the door in order to make an extra sale. It's a short-term approach that leads to a long-term struggle.

IT'S OK TO BUCK THE TREND

There are hundreds of restaurants in Lake Como, Italy. Most of them are close to the lake, beautiful with a decadent fit-out, serve great food and have many signature dishes. They compete with each other pretty fiercely over who has the nicest decor, cleanest white linen and best views of the lake.

Then there's a funny place located one mile inland. It has no views, and features plastic white chairs, old tablecloths, cheaply laminated menus and pretty average service. To top it all off, their menu only has one thing: the best pizza you've ever tasted.

This restaurant, called Tremesso, is full almost every night of the week. Millionaire tourists venture from all sides of the lake to get there, then wind their way up the dark roads into the local village to try and find this little pizza restaurant run by a husband and wife team (he's in the kitchen, and she serves the tables).

The restaurant is in their back garden surrounded by their plants. They grow tomatoes, onions, herbs and spices. They make their own pizza dough, sun-dry their own tomatoes, crush their own garlic and chop their own basil.

They are different than the region's countless other eateries for several reasons. They aren't playing the same game as the other restaurants; they open up their home and their garden to their guests and they grow their own fresh ingredients. Above all, they get *one thing* right – the pizza.

And their pizza is to die for. The base is paper thin and perfectly crisp and the topping is thick, fresh and packed full of garlic. The pizza is wood fired for the exact right amount of time so that it's crispy and smoky but not blackened. It arrives on the table steaming hot with local cheeses running off the sides.

This place is memorable and remarkable for all the right reasons. You feel compelled to tell others about it. I'm sure that this couple hasn't read a single book on marketing, but there's a lot to be learned from them. The main lesson is that it's OK to play a different game to everyone else. It's

OK to be old-fashioned when everyone else is trying to be modern; it's OK to be expensive when everyone else is trying to be cheap; it's OK to be flamboyant when everyone else is trying to fit in.

What are the expected norms in your industry? What's everyone else doing? What would the opposite be and how would you do that really well?

If everyone in your industry charges by the hour, create a fixed price solution. If everyone in your industry sells components, be the company that only sells bundles. If everyone is showing off about their heritage, be the company that is a new and disruptive thought leader. If the industry norm is to sign clients on to a 12-month contract, be the first to offer month-by-month billing with no break clause.

VALUE IS CREATED IN THE ECOSYSTEM

Life isn't simple and neither is business. Nothing works on its own; everything works together. Gone are the days when providing great value gets you paid well. The people who get paid well today are the people who build a sophisticated product and services ecosystem.

Consider where famous chef, Jamie Oliver, makes his money. Is it the TV shows, the recipe books, the supermarket sponsorships or his chain of restaurants?

Oliver does make some money from appearances BUT sometimes he turns up to speak at important conferences like 'TED' for free. He spends hours on Twitter and gives away so much value online BUT he's not getting paid to do it. He's regarded as a great businessman BUT he spends a lot of time working on charitable projects. He sells a lot of books BUT he spends millions on PR. You may wonder – is it worth it?

The truth is, it's all part of an ecosystem of products and services that all work together to make a lot of money and to have a big impact. It's the ecosystem as a whole that creates the value, NOT any one product, service, system or person.

You can't try to take the ecosystem apart and measure it in isolation. The books in isolation might seem like a waste of time; however, maybe the books are what make the restaurants so popular. You might think he's overpaid for his sponsorship deals – but when you consider what he's paying for PR, it might be fair value.

None of it works on its own; all of it works together. Your job is to create a remarkable ecosystem that delivers a positive experience and keeps people coming back for more.

Contrast Oliver's approach with that of most business managers and owners I meet. Many are annoyed because their business isn't simple. They say to me things like:

"I deliver great value and I expect to get paid for it. What's wrong with that?"

"They should pay me my fees if they want me to come and speak at their conference. I can't be expected to work for nothing!"

"This social media stuff is a waste of time. It takes hours and I'm not getting paid to do it!"

"I will do something for charity after I make money. I don't have spare cash to be giving away; my business needs it!"

These sentiments make perfect sense in a highly simplified world. But that's not the world we live in.

Every business leader must acknowledge that their job is to make a highly complex system seem effortless. They must turn chaos into order and do it with style. Entrepreneurs and leaders cannot simply shoot to deliver value and then get fairly rewarded. That model died a long time ago. Today's high-performing businesses are ecosystems of people, products and services that are all working in harmony. They are complex, paradoxical and hard to mimic.

You cannot expect to be highly rewarded for doing a good job. Rather, you can expect to be rewarded when you've built a high-performing ecosystem that delivers value. You'll stay oversubscribed when you've built something people feel part of that leaves them uplifted.

GIVE AWAY IDEAS – CHARGE FOR IMPLEMENTATION

As a child, I remember my dad's office was full of white cassette tapes in colourful laminated boxes with photos of men in suits on the front. He had tapes on goal setting, marketing, time management and relationships. These tapes weren't cheap in the 80s and 90s; in fact each set cost hundreds of dollars.

It was the information age and information was highly valuable and difficult to come by. Finding someone who would share *quality* ideas was even harder. Gurus in all industries sold special reports, audio seminars, documents, subscriptions and workbooks by the truckload. There was a sense of anxiety during that time that someone else might have access to more information than you and you'd miss out on something great because you were off doing something else.

Then something changed. Google, YouTube, Wordpress, iTunes came along and suddenly everyone was drowning in information. By 2010 the amount of readily accessible and free information you could get your hands on was endless. You could download any document you wanted, find any fact at the touch of a button, watch endless hours of video on any topic and listen to terabytes of high-quality audio podcasts for free.

After 2010, the anxiety people felt was a sense that they had *too much* information coming at them and not enough time to do anything with it. The *value* of information has fallen through the floor and the value of getting things done has risen through the roof.

These days, my dad's office is clutter free. He's got a few of his favourite books, but other than that, he wants to avoid distractions so he can run his business. When he needs information, he simply goes online.

This isn't obvious to some people though. They are still under the impression that their information is somehow more valuable and they should make money from it. I see plenty of people still trying to make money from ebooks, downloads and audio programmes. They refuse to acknowledge the world has changed.

The new model is pretty simple though and only requires a small shift. You must give away information freely or cheaply and then charge for the *implementation* work.

I share my ideas freely in books and blogs. I rarely hold anything back; if I have a good idea it goes up for the world to see. As a result, people read my ideas and then want to put them into action. I often get emails from people who have a budget to get my company to help them implement the ideas.

You can see this happening successfully with many large companies. High-end yoga apparel brand lululemon has a ton of information about yoga on their website. You can read, listen to, watch or do things on their site for days. You can even go into the retail store and take a free yoga class. When the time comes that you want to get active with your yoga you then go shopping with them and buy the kit you need.

Consider the spectrum of value your business could offer:

1 **Information or ideas** – People are drowning in ideas, information, recipes and strategies. You could give people the blueprints for a stealth bomber these days and they would lose it in their "downloads" folder. Information and ideas are good to give to potential clients to demonstrate that your company is a thought leader; the days of trading on ideas and information are numbered. Example: a diet and fitness plan.

2 **Components** – This is where you sell the "building blocks" that people need to create something themselves. Components could be raw materials, basic services or regular commodities. You'll need to sell a lot of these if you want to make any money. Example: a set of workout weights.

3 **Supervision** – This is the lowest form of implementation work you can offer. It's where your company provides close and ongoing supervision while your client works at achieving an outcome. Be aware you're dangerously close to selling ideas unless you're taking an active role on the client's ongoing journey and assisting them to get the results they want. If there's no real accountability or personalization, this type of implementation will lose its value. Example: a gym.

4 **Done with you** – This is of moderate value to your clients. It's where you and your clients work together to create an outcome. They provide some of the work and so does your business. Example: a personal fitness trainer.

5 **Done for you** – This is a "solution" whereby your business has created a full and complete answer to a problem that your client needs solved. This is the most valuable solution for a customer because it involves very little of their time or creative energy to get a result. Example: liposuction.

The more your business takes on the responsibility of delivering an outcome, with little or no external input, the more value it creates. We see solution products in a variety of industries, from telecommunications, software, accommodation, financial services and countless others. These solutions are ready to go; you can buy them and no further input is required from you in order for them to be implemented.

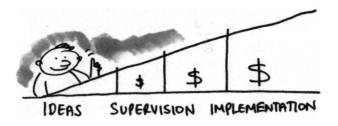

And almost every industry offers various products at all levels. The less energy required from the client, the more valuable the product. Sticking with the example from above, if you want to lose weight, you can buy a book for $20, pay $500 for a gym membership, $3,000 for personal training or $15,000 for liposuction.

Your business should offer several products and cover all of these categories. It should be part of an ecosystem of products and services.

You must remain conscious that the value has shifted away from information and into implementation. Don't go broke trying to sell information; make millions giving it away for free and then charging to make it happen.

IT'S EASIER TO CLIMB SMALL STAIRS THAN TO JUMP BIG WALLS

It was just after the dot-com crash in 2001 and investors were gun shy. They had lost a lot of money on technology companies and they didn't want to lose any more. So the timing couldn't be worse for Matthew Michalewicz, a young entrepreneur who needed to raise $3m to launch a very powerful IT business with a sound business plan. Just a few months earlier, investors had been beating down his door and would have transferred funds after reading the business plan. Now everything was quiet.

But Matthew had an idea. Rather than asking investors for funds, he would show them the plan and ask them for an "expression of interest form". The form indicated that they liked the plan and wanted more information as it unfolded. Along with the expression of interest, he asked them to indicate an amount they might feel comfortable investing in this sort of business. He made it clear that there was no obligation to invest; it was just an indication.

After six weeks, Matthew had expressions of interest for more than $4 million. He was oversubscribed. He then decided to call everyone on the list and let them know that he only wanted to raise $3 million but he had expressions of interest from investors for $1 million more than he planned to raise. He asked each investor whether they would be willing to put some of the money in that they had indicated.

All of the investors started to put in the full amounts that they had indicated. He had raised the full amount before he called back the whole list.

Had Matthew gone to the investors asking for money up front, he likely would have gotten a lot of "nos". No one was investing so soon after the crash. But because he created an easy first step, he was able to get soft commitments that he then firmed up after being sure he was oversubscribed.

This isn't just a good idea in times of caution and austerity. This strategy fits with human behaviour at the best of times too. Making people jump over the wall freezes people into inaction. People hate making big commitments or taking any action that's hard to back out from. Giving people a low-risk first step is a powerful way to move people in the right direction.

Not so long ago, a consultant approached my business with a remarkable plan. She had 20+ years of experience developing systems and rolling out operations with a global business that I admired. She knew answers to all sorts of questions that I had; she was smart, experienced and I was thrilled by the idea of working with her after the first meeting.

A week later, upon my request, she sent a plan to work together with a six-figure estimate. I agreed with the value she offered and that she was the person best suited to help us – but I was reluctant to commit to such a sum of money as a first deal. To this day, we've not moved forward because the decision was too big for my team to proceed. Had she created a low-risk first step for us to climb we would have spent a fortune by now. Giving us a wall to climb killed the sale.

INNOVATE – BUT DON'T MESS WITH A WINNING FORMULA

Singer Alicia Keys made a terrible mistake when she tweeted from her iPhone – a mistake that could have been one of the nails in the coffin for Blackberry. Quite separately from the content of the tweet, a message was sent to the world that even Blackberry's company ambassador preferred an Apple product.

Only weeks earlier, Blackberry's maker RIM had signed a deal with Keys to try and make them appear cool. Blackberry executives had clearly felt the pinch from iPhone and they started to forget their winning formula. They made the decision to try and beat Apple at its own game – which from a distance seemed like an insane move.

Blackberry brought Keys in to help design a sexy and sleek new device and to tell the world that Blackberry was the phone she owned. Except for one thing – she didn't. She owned an iPhone as everyone could see for themselves on the meta tags in her tweets.

Years earlier, Blackberry had risen to dominance with a clear winning formula: people don't buy a Blackberry; they get them from their companies. Blackberry phones were safe, secure and compatible. They were hard to hack and easy for a central IT department to lock down. Members of IT departments recommended Blackberry not because it was cool, but because it fit with their systems. No amount of glamour and fanfare for iPhone was going to change the mind of a CTO who had to buy and manage thousands of handsets for an army of workers.

Secure, safe and compatible is a winning formula that could have kept RIM in business for many years – if only they'd stuck to it. Cool, sleek and aspirational was Apple's winning formula and no one in their right mind should try to compete with Apple on their home turf.

Companies that succeed innovate BUT they never mess with their winning formula.

Porsche innovates all the time, but they don't alter what has always worked for them. Their frog-looking 911 range was gorgeous in 1963 and it's still gorgeous today. Decade upon decade, they don't look too dissimilar to their predecessors. Porsche knows that their design isn't broken and that's not where they make radical changes.

The musical, *Les Misérables*, has been running in London for over 25 years almost unchanged. Every showing is near full and the tickets aren't cheap. The cast and crew change from time to time, but the music, the characters and even most of the marketing stays the same. It would be easy for creative types to make changes, but it takes discipline to leave it alone and make changes only where needed.

LEGO has extended their brand and partnered with others in highly innovative ways over the years. But the one thing they stay true to is their LEGO brick system; it's the core of who they are and they know not to mess with it. Expectant mums and dads all over the world look forward to playing with LEGO when their child is old enough. The magic would be lost if the bricks were somehow different to the ones they had when they were kids. A little bit of remaining tradition can be a welcome thing in a world of rapid change.

In business schools around the world, the word "innovation" is sacrosanct. You can't go wrong talking about "innovation": it's the one thing anyone can talk about and get unanimous agreement. Sometimes however, innovation isn't what a business needs. And that is certainly the case if it requires them to alter what works.

If you know your winning formula, innovate at the edges and keep focused on the core. Innovating out of a sense of boredom is dangerous. You might be bored, but the market may still be in love with what you do.

The Foo Fighters might get sick of their own songs but they know their fans aren't. They know that everyone goes to a Foo Fighters concert and wants to hear the song "Everlong". They can play new music, but they can't leave the stadium without playing the songs everyone came to hear.

Roger Federer is probably a bit sick of tennis; maybe he's even bored of winning by now (though probably not). He likely has days when he'd love to go play golf or try basketball. But now's not the time to switch games; now is the time to enjoy the benefits of all the hard work he put in as a child and cement his place as one of the greatest players of all time.

There is a steak restaurant in Melbourne, Australia called Vlados. On the walls you'll see photos of the world's most powerful people: celebrities, politicians, billionaires and royals have all had dinner there. Sitting amongst the photos is a small plaque that says "Celebrating no change for 30 years". They've had the same menu, the same staff and the same formula for success for three decades. When you're onto a winner, don't mess with it too much.

NOTHING BEATS BEING POSITIVELY REMARKABLE

If people talk about you in a positive way, your marketing budget reduces to zero.

REPLACE YOUR MARKETING BUDGET WITH A REMARKABLE BUDGET

Traditional marketing and advertising is not as important as it once was. What matters most, now and in the future, is having a product that is worth talking about.

We have a smart phone in our pocket and every friend we've ever met on our social media directories just waiting to offer up welcomed advice. Add to that, we can see user reviews, blogs, star ratings and other relevant data in a dozen different ways.

The problem with traditional marketing in the current climate: you might be marketing your competition!

Imagine an electronics company takes out an ad in the paper that says "Take Amazing Photos with Our New Digital SLR". You read the ad and remember that you have a holiday coming up that will provide some awesome photo opportunities. Your next move is where everything goes wrong for the poor electronics company who splashed out on advertising. Instead of going to their store, you open up a browser on your iPhone, Google "Digital SLR Camera" and start looking at reviews.

You discover that there is an amazing online warehouse that everyone is raving about, that sells cameras at "factory direct prices" online. You also discover that a leading blogger on photography is recommending people buy a different brand of camera that is not the one in the ad.

You post a tweet on Twitter "I'm buying a #DSLR #camera. Any #advice?" Your friends tweet back and point you to a number of great deals. By now you have forgotten that the only reason you began thinking of buying a camera was because of the ad you saw.

The advertiser will pay to get you thinking – but you will probably buy the product that is the most "remarkable". And being remarkable is NOT about offering stupid gimmicks or pointless stunts. It's about being the best in your niche or micro-niche, offering genuine advantages, real benefits and a superior experience. Most of all, it's about authentically caring about what you do and being in a class of your own.

This also doesn't just mean being premium or high end. You can be remarkable for your innovative approach or your remarkably fair deals. You could be remarkably cheap if that's your point of difference or remarkable for the lengths you'll go to please a customer.

When someone asks "Who should I buy from?" it is your name that should come up. *That's* remarkable.

Your businesses must begin investing more money into your products and your customer service and less money into advertising and traditional forms of marketing. Oversubscribed businesses spend money on their existing customers before they spend money on their prospective ones. It seems counter-intuitive – but if you get it right, your existing customers go out and do your marketing *for* you.

I would go as far to say you should take at least 50% of your traditional marketing budget and transfer it to the "being remarkable" budget. If you do, your products will sell because other people will spend money on marketing and then people find you.

BUILD A REMARKABLY TRUSTED PERSONAL BRAND

Richard Branson steps out of the car and the media photographers go into a frenzy. He's dressed as an Indian chief and he's carrying a small axe. He makes his way up to the CEO of Sydney airport, extends his hand and says, "I'm here to bury the hatchet."

In that moment, the details of the conflict become irrelevant and all is instantly forgiven. Richard Branson has used his personal brand to instantly resolve a standoff between two companies who couldn't find their common ground when it came to airport terminal allocation. His top executives had tried their hardest to get Virgin into the main terminal of the airport and had been very publically rejected. In the end it was a magic touch from Richard that got the deal done.

Whatever the situation, Branson is acutely aware that his own personal brand wields the power to get things done at lightning speed. He uses his brand to resolve conflicts, to launch products, to raise capital, to attract talented leaders and to effect social change.

Branson has authored and released seven books. He writes articles for newspapers and has a team of content-marketing experts who manage his social media profiles. Sufficed to say, he's mastered the art of capturing the media's attention. He's built a brand that attracts opportunities constantly and he's so well liked and trusted that his involvement in a venture can make it an overnight success.

Gone are the days when a company of any size can survive as a faceless corporation that exists as a set of logos, colours, symbols and sounds. Nowadays, bands live and die by the personalities that represent them. Today people want to know who the founder is, the CEO's background and what sort of beliefs the leading executives hold. Companies that become oversubscribed build and leverage the personal brands of the people who are inside.

You build a personal brand when you or your people become better known, liked and trusted in your market. You can build personal brands using videos, blogs, articles, books, photos, quotes, live appearances, talks, publicity and events.

Personal brands are powerful for a few reasons.

Firstly, human brains are highly geared to connect with people. A big brand can spend millions trying to get you to recognize their symbol, but it's far easier to get people to recognize a face. Humans are hard wired to trust and connect with faces, voices, body language and words directly from a person. We are geared to associate with people and to talk about them. If you build a remarkably trusted personal brand, people will naturally recommend you.

Secondly, a personal brand ensures that "you" are in the room when you're not actually in the room. That brand is present every time people mention you or discuss what you would do in the circumstances. But in order for that to happen, people need to know your unique take on things. Having a remarkably trusted personal brand means that things happen the way you'd want them to happen, even when you aren't there to make them happen.

Finally, you get to keep your brand for as long as you live (maybe even after you're gone). Even if you sell a business or change career, a strong personal brand will give you a flying head start into the next endeavour.

Rob Gardner is regarded as one of the most influential people in the pension fund industry worldwide. He left his high paying job at Merrill Lynch to set up his own boutique firm with a mission to help solve the pension fund crisis that exists in most developed countries. Gardner's previous corporate employers expected him to be a faceless "asset" who built the company brand and never his own. At his own company, Reddington, he's made some changes to that plan. His goal is to build a company that is full of key people of influence. He's set up a company blog where every employee is requested to blog each month and share their ideas under their own name. Each person in the business is encouraged to learn how to pitch the vision of the business to others, to go online and build connections with people. In this way, Rob Gardner is building a company full of personalities.

This strategy has led to fast growth and big partnerships. His business is punching high above its weight and winning deals over rivals who have millions to spend on marketing and branding a faceless facade.

What's more is that he's attracting top talent because great people don't want to be kept in the dark anymore. High performers want to build up the company brand as well as their own. Encouraging people to become known liked and trusted helps you, helps them, and it allows you to have a steady stream of high performers who aspire to join your team.

A lot of people have a fear of putting themselves out there. But you'll need to weigh it up against your fear of being a faceless, generic business that isn't oversubscribed. When you examine the full picture, you'll see that it's worth building a brand because it's one of the fastest ways to stay oversubscribed with everything you do.

Test yourself as a key person of influence: www. keypersonofinfluence.com/scorecard

Part II

The Campaign Driven Enterprise Method: Turning Principles into Strategy

I t's time to take the powerful ideas we've discussed so far and formulate a strategy.

Thinking Like a Campaign Driven Enterprise

In any given industry some people struggle to get enough customers while others have more than they can handle. In any given market, some companies chase for clients while others select who they want to work with and turn away the rest.

What sets these two groups apart is the way they see themselves. It's the difference between seeing yourself as running a "business" (which actually sounds a lot like busyness) and a "Campaign Driven Enterprise".

A Campaign Driven Enterprise is the identity you'll need to adopt in order to become oversubscribed. It's a strategic mindset that focuses you on running powerful campaigns. It turns your business into a series of critical moments and important events.

Consider the way the engine of a car hums along. If you look closely, you notice that hum is a series of well-timed revolutions. In the same way a business that is humming along is often a series of well-timed campaigns.

Great companies – like Nike, Apple and Virgin, for example – all started (and continue to thrive) using campaigns. It's also how I was able to launch a business at age 22 and make over one million dollars in the first 12 months. It's how we then went on to do that with five other businesses in both boom times and in the recession.

The skills and strategies for running a Campaign Driven Enterprise are transferable. In fact, the key to scaling your business depends on you learning them.

However, most businesses don't think like this. They are set up to win and service clients one at a time. This approach is both unsustainable and causes people to grow bored or to burn out. This doesn't work for the business owner or employees who exhaust themselves quickly and can't scale, and it doesn't work for the clients who don't get the attention they deserve. It's incredibly difficult to create the sales velocity required for fast growth without thinking like a campaign-driven enterprise.

I have never gone out to get one customer at a time. I run events and promotions that encourage everyone to come to us all at once. I want people to feel a buzz and an excitement! Sitting with one potential customer at a time kills the energy for me, the team and the clients. Every entrepreneur, leader or marketing manager must learn how to encourage 10, 20 or even hundreds of people at one time to engage with their business.

This section of the book moves us from principles into planning. It's time to take the powerful ideas we've discussed so far and formulate a strategy. Becoming oversubscribed isn't something you can do on the fly; it takes preparation and strategy executed with precision. Your goal is to stop behaving like a business and become a campaign-driven enterprise with a goal to becoming oversubscribed.

Admittedly, it does feel safer to do things in a linear way, or one at a time. You go and meet a potential client, you sell something to them, you deliver it, you go and meet another potential client; this seems natural, and logical.

But that's not how a campaign-driven enterprise thinks. Instead they look to cluster activities up into larger chunks. They go and get 100 potential clients, choose the twenty they want to work with, deliver an experience to those twenty – and then they go get 100 more potential clients.

I challenge you to let go of the linear world where things happen in order, one-at-a-time and to embrace a little bit more chaos where things move in waves.

The ideas and methods I'm going to share in this section are easy to get excited about; however, their implementation is what trips many people up. You will need to stick to a plan and to do the work to execute each step with all the focus, commitment and excellence of a professional athlete.

Regardless of whether you're an architect, artist, inventor, software developer, public speaker or high-end corporate consultant, the fundamental principles that make a campaign-driven enterprise successful are applicable across all levels and industries. Whether you're B2B or B2C or both, integrating a campaign methodology into your 12-month plan will drive growth faster than you could imagine.

To make it easier, I'm going to outline a specific method for becoming oversubscribed. It's a framework for implementing your ideas in a logical sequence.

THE CAMPAIGN DRIVEN ENTERPRISE METHOD

The method is broken into five phases:

PHASE 1: PLANNING

You must know your "capacity" and who it's for – that is, know the point where you'll actually be oversubscribed and who will see the most value in that capacity. Design your campaigns and set a 12-month rolling campaign schedule.

PHASE 2: BUILD-UP

Share genuine insights that lead people to conclude that they desire to work with you, or entertain them sufficiently so that they desire to continue the relationship.

PHASE 3: OVERSUBSCRIBED RELEASE

After you've sufficiently built interest, you can announce that you are able to release your product or service and allow selected people to buy.

PHASE 4: REMARKABLE DELIVERY

Surprise and delight your clients above and beyond their expectations, leaving them feeling uplifted.

PHASE 5: INNOVATE AND CELEBRATE

Tell the stories, share the numbers, issue reports, capture the magic moments and spread the word about your campaign's achievements. Learn the lessons, make changes and refine the process before repeating it.

Is this the only method to become oversubscribed? No.

The most powerful way to become oversubscribed is to be utterly remarkable in everything you do. Invest thousands of hours in becoming the most visible, valuable, noteworthy, raw talent in your industry. If you're at that level, you'll always be oversubscribed.

There are also plenty of people who've done it with luck. There are products that are genuinely so timely they sell off the shelves, ideas that tap into the zeitgeist, trends that spring up unpredictably or resources that come along through pure good fortune.

There are many ways to get a successful result. This method however, is one that works for most people most of the time, and allows you to evaluate where to focus your attention. It doesn't require you to be unimaginably talented or lucky; but it does help you improve and challenges you to be your best.

Let's explore this method step by step.

CAMPAIGN PLANNING: KNOW YOUR CAPACITY, WHO IT'S FOR AND WHEN YOU CAN DELIVER IT

How many remarkable client relationships can you have? How many epic products can you sell? How many hours can you deliver truly great work?

Most people love to answer that question with, "As many as people will buy!" However, that simply isn't true. The truth is your capacity is limited. Even software is limited by the market size, the number of supporting devices and the supporting infrastructure.

So why do people pretend that they have no issues with capacity? Why pretend that you can serve everyone when you can't?

It's far better to figure out how many people you can properly serve and then be honest about that number. If your business can only take good care of 21 clients a year, then say so. If you're only comfortable taking on 10,455 subscribers to your newsletter, then say so. If you're maxed out with 283 restaurant bookings a week, then be clear about it.

Knowing your real capacity is powerful. It's almost impossible to become oversubscribed if you don't know what your capacity is.

Guy Rigby is the head of the Entrepreneurship Division at the accounting firm Smith & Williamson. When I referred someone to him he said, "I don't have the capacity to bring on board more clients until next quarter." He explained to me that his team limited the number of new clients each quarter so that they never risk the quality of their service. He was genuine and sure enough he made me wait three months before I could recommend a client to the firm. Rigby knows his capacity and sticks to it.

Every business has a capacity to deliver a remarkable product or service. Once you try to exceed that capacity, your standards across the board have to drop and people don't get the experience they thought they were going to get. Not just the new clients – all of them. They feel disappointed, and it's a slippery slope from there. This business will suffer as people learn about your customers' underwhelming experiences.

So let's take another look at your business' capacity to deliver. How many clients can you *truly* serve well? How many products can you really sell? How many customers can you genuinely make feel uplifted?

IT BEGINS WITH A HAPPY CUSTOMER

I want you to imagine your perfect client. This person is perfect in every way – enjoyable to work with, they pay on time, they tell their friends about you and they come back wanting more. You enjoy working with them and they think the world of you.

What is it about the person that makes them so perfect?

Let's go back to the time before this person became your client. What were they looking to achieve? What problem were they trying to solve? What was less than perfect in their world?

Every business exists to solve problems for its customers. The reason your perfect clients love you is because you solve a high value problem for them in a remarkable way. You meet an unmet need; you scratch an itch; you leave them feeling an emotion they hadn't felt elsewhere.

Unless you can understand this unmet need and what the problem is that you solve for your perfect client you can never generate one.

So let's take a look at the problem you solve for people. High value products and services are linked to four underlying drivers:

1 Save or make money.
2 Save time or eliminate wastage.
3 Bring increased emotional benefits.
4 Ease pain, suffering or negative emotions.

To use an example, let's examine all the reasons why someone would buy a Rolex watch. This is a great example because it seems on the surface like such a strange thing to purchase. A Rolex only has one function, it's five hundred times more expensive than a viable alternative, and it's heavier and more uncomfortable to wear than other watches. To top it all off, if you need to know the time you can just look at your phone, which most people do multiple times a day now anyway. So why do so many people still buy Rolex watches?

1 **To save or make money** – Some people buy a Rolex for a business associate or high performing staff member as a gift. A $10,000 watch is impressive and has more impact than a $20,000 cash bonus. Some people use it as a reward for the top person on a sales team, which motivates people to hit targets. Some people wear them to communicate status, which allows them to charge a higher price for their services or win bigger deals.

2 **To save time** – A Rolex saves some wearers a lot of time. For people who meet new people on a regular basis a Rolex helps to communicate to a person you've only just met that you've achieved success in the past and you're confident that you can do it again.

3 **To bring increased emotional benefits** – A Rolex can have many emotional benefits linked to it. Many people buy a Rolex to celebrate a milestone or an achievement. Each time the wearer looks at the time they are reminded of that achievement. It might also be a gift for a loved one

that communicates something special between the two parties.

4 **To ease pain, suffering or negative emotions** – Finally, some people buy themselves a Rolex because they feel unrewarded, unrecognized or unappreciated and they want something that makes them feel special. The purchase is designed to alleviate the negative feelings they have and replace them with a set of positive emotions.

When we examine the purchase of an expensive Rolex through these four drivers, it suddenly makes total sense. A watch isn't just a device to tell the time, it's a device to save or make money, save time, bring emotional benefits or alleviate negative emotions or pain.

ACTIVITY 1

Explore several of your recent purchases and list the underlying drivers behind why you purchased them. What compelled you to buy certain gadgets, entertainment, holidays or new clothing? Find the link between your buying behaviour and these four underlying drivers.

ACTIVITY 2

Looking at the four underlying drivers, can you honestly say your product does this too?

How does your product save or make people more money?

_____   _____

_____   _____

How does your product save time or eliminate wastage?

_____   _____

_____   _____

How does your product deliver greater emotional benefits than other products?

_____   _____

_____   _____

How does your product remove pain or negative emotions?

_____   _____

_____   _____

If you can genuinely link your product to the four underlying drivers, you'll have a deeper insight into why people buy from you – and you can position your products to be more highly valued.

This also adds a dimension to your understanding of your "capacity". Rather than thinking about your capacity to ship a product, facilitate a download, deliver a service or produce a widget, you should now be considering your capacity to leave someone feeling delighted.

The thing that matters when it comes to capacity is your ability to leave people uplifted as a result of doing business with you. If a person leaves your business in the same or worse emotional state than they arrived, you didn't deliver. And every time you let someone down, you put your business at risk.

Sure, Apple could ship more phones if they didn't charge the battery in the factory; but it would disappoint customers to open the box and find out that they couldn't turn on their new phone. When Apple thinks about its capacity, it needs to include the time taken to charge the battery before it ships.

A fine restaurant could rush you to leave after you've finished your meal, but it's unlikely you'd tell your friends to go there. When a restaurant thinks about capacity, they need to factor in the lingering conversations people have after they finish their meal.

A top nightclub could cram people in who haven't put effort into their fashion. They could have people standing shoulder to shoulder in line at the bar. But if they did that, it wouldn't be a top nightclub for very long. When a top nightclub thinks about capacity, they need to think about how many people fit in the club so that everyone is having a good time.

What did you do to make your customers so happy? What ingredients go into leaving someone uplifted?

When you understand the ingredients for creating a delighted customer, you can then work backwards from there and calculate your current capacity to make someone feel that way.

WHO'S YOUR MARKET?

Becoming oversubscribed is about finding a market that highly values you, has the capacity to pay you, and that you want to serve.

This combination is important, even two out of three won't work. If they highly value you and you like them but they don't have any money to pay you, you'll eventually go broke. If they have the capacity to pay you and they highly value you but you don't fancy working in this market, you'll get bored or frustrated before success blossoms. If they could pay you and you like this market but they don't value you, you'll struggle to get clients.

That is why you need all three.

David Boucher has created some of the most expensive furniture on the planet. He sells writing desks that start at $80,000, tables for $200,000 and even a chess set for $18,000. His furniture often sells for more money second-hand than new.

His company, Boucher & Co., is the only company on earth who are commissioned to provide a custom interior for a Rolls Royce. From his workshop in Toowoomba,

Australia, David and his craftsmen build these pieces and sell them to millionaires and billionaires worldwide. There's a waiting list for his furniture despite the astronomical prices (a dining table and chairs can cost north of $200k!).

David couldn't sell this furniture to the typical IKEA furniture buyer. If he tried to attract that market, he'd be very disappointed and might even start to doubt his abilities. Fortunately, he's found the right market for his products and he's oversubscribed in that market. The billionaires he sells to admire his work, have the capacity to pay for his modern art deco designs and David enjoys serving this market.

Conversely, I know of a frustrated yoga instructor who's regarded highly as a top trained practitioner but consistently fails to get people to attend her classes. Her studio is based in a lower income area, but she's trying to charge a fee most of the people who live there simply cannot afford. But since she regards people in the wealthier areas as snobby, she doesn't want to set up a studio in that area.

Her formula is broken. People in her area might value her but they don't have the capacity to pay her rates, and she doesn't feel drawn to work with the people who do. As such, she will struggle to become oversubscribed if she can't find a market that values her, can pay her and that she wants to work with.

ACTIVITY: WHO'S YOUR MARKET?

Who has the capacity to pay you?

_____

_____

What would they highly value from you?

_____

_____

What about these people makes you feel drawn to working
with them?

_____

_____

CLIENTS VERSUS CUSTOMERS

A customer buys something. A client keeps coming back. A
customer results from a transaction whereas a client results
from a relationship.

Your job is to create both. Your business will need to
offer products and services at a lower price point so that
people can try you out and you can see if they are right for
you too. For example, your business might run a promotional
event and 100 people buy a ticket for $40. These people are
customers of your business because they bought something.

You might then decide that you'd be happy to work with
20 out of the 100 on an ongoing basis. Of these 20, you sign
on 10 new clients who will buy from you regularly because
you nurture the relationship.

You wouldn't have found those 10 clients if you hadn't
generated 100 customers first. You need to generate *plenty*
of customers who buy a "product-for-prospects" at a low-
risk price point. You then need to discern who would be a
great client for you long term.

A barber shop might have 1,000 *customers* a year who step in for a cut once or twice. They will also have a group of *clients* who get their hair cut at the same place every month. The barber shop is wise to be able to know the difference between the two. They will also be wise to know how to turn good customers into raving fan clients.

There's nothing wrong with having a purely transactional interaction with people if the terms are clear. They buy your product, it's great, and they are happy customers. Ultimately though, the only way to sustain your business is if some of these happy customers become happy clients.

For this reason, you'll need to create at least two types of products:

1. A **product-for-prospects:** Aimed at generating lots of happy customers.
2. A **core offering:** A full and remarkable client relationship that evolves over time.

GETTING A GRIP ON REALITY

I recently spoke to someone who had the idea to publish books online about how to invest in industry property. He wanted to sell the books for £39 each and thought it would be great to sell 100 copies per month and make passive income. However, his plan wasn't working. The site had received a meagre few downloads and more than half the people wanted to activate the 100% money back guarantee.

When I asked him if this product would leave people delighted, he went off on a big spiel about how delighted people would be if they could see a financial future for themselves, how much time his book would save people, how much money his book would make them and so forth.

I responded by saying that I had reservations. I explained that there are thousands of property books on Amazon that mostly all say the same things as his book. Additionally, there's a ton of free books, free videos, free membership sites, free events and free podcasts on this topic. All of them are produced by people who claim to be property experts, so why would I want to pay £39 for another book on the topic? If anything, I would feel annoyed that I had paid for something that I could get for free.

He responded by saying, "Lots of people don't know they can get that stuff for free. I'm targeting people who don't already read those kinds of books."

I indicated my concern that at some point after reading his book, people discover the book was overpriced and they want their money back.

He responded by saying "They should be grateful that I got them into the industry and without me they wouldn't have made a start. They should be grateful I took the time to write the book!" To which I replied, "People don't work like that."

This sort of conversation isn't uncommon. I see business owners who are trying to convince others why they should be delighted rather than acknowledging that they aren't. Your goal isn't to *tell people why they should be delighted*; your goal is to watch and see if people ARE delighted after doing business with you. If they aren't, then you have a problem – and no amount of explaining why they *should be* will change the fact that they aren't.

It's not the customer's job to fix it: they're either happy or they aren't, they saw value or they didn't. They might be able to tell you what they wanted to be different but it's your job to figure out a solution.

I know of another property business that gives away its content – books, videos, resources and reports – for free. It tells people about hot locations and market trends. It then works to build their clients a property portfolio, renovate their properties and rent them out for a top price. This company isn't focused on passive income. This company is focused on delighting everyone who they come in contact with – the readers, the property buyers and the renters.

Your job is to keep focusing on creating a delighted customer. Crack the code on what constitutes value for them and how best to deliver that.

Stay curious and focused on the reality of the situation. Don't see the world as you'd like it to be; see what's really going on and be willing to make changes until your customers leave feeling uplifted.

ACTIVITY

What negative feedback does your business typically get?

_____

_____

What less than positive things might people be saying behind your back?

_____

_____

How could you change things so your business delights people?

_____

_____

THE REAL NUMBER

Now you're looking at your business through different eyes. What's your current capacity to create a delighted client?

I've done this activity with some people and their answer is zero. They currently do not have the capacity to leave anyone feeling delighted. The goal for their business is to get the capacity to make one person feel great about doing business with them.

Don't feel discouraged if you're in that camp. In fact, you should get excited, because your mission is clear: uplift one person as a result of doing business with you. On the flip side, I've worked with large companies that already have thousands of clients who have to get honest about the number of people who are satisfied versus delighted. A large company's job isn't just to sell more stuff. It's to leave more people delighted. So, a big company might need to start with a number like 10,000 and work to increase that number to 12,000 over a year.

Remember, knowing your capacity is about knowing how many people you can delight.

I'VE ONLY GOT THREE LEFT

So – what's your number? How many people do you have the capacity to delight in the year ahead?

YOUR SCHEDULE FOR BECOMING OVERSUBSCRIBED

I stood in the kitchen of a multi-million dollar, waterfront mansion. On the designer granite bench was a massive chart of the year ahead that my mentor was using to plan the next 12 months of campaigns.

He started by putting in his holidays. He blocked out a skiing trip with his family, a sailing trip with his friends and several romantic weekends with his wife. Then he blocked out his training and development. He had booked several courses and trainings that he wanted to attend and complete. He put in training days with his team and planning days for his leaders that occurred every quarter.

He said to me, "Training and development is key. Depending on how fast you want to grow, you must commit to spending 5–15% of your income on high-quality training and development so you're always at the cutting edge."

Once he had the big stuff blocked out, he looked at his sales targets. He knew his numbers and amounts of sales he would need to have a year of prosperity and growth. He then devised campaigns every month and every quarter of the year ahead. He had a Valentine's Day campaign, an Easter campaign, a summer campaign and a Christmas campaign – among others. Every month, he had a plan for how he would drive his business so that he would stay oversubscribed.

When you break it down over time, your capacity number might be 10 per month or 150 per quarter.

Staying oversubscribed requires that you're constantly planning your campaigns a year in advance. You need to know how many customers you can delight and *when* you can delight them. In order to achieve this goal, you need to be thinking months ahead *at all times*. A powerful campaign needs time to build up momentum. If you don't allow enough time, there simply isn't enough energy built up to create a rush of buyers.

You now know the capacity of clients you want to achieve in the year ahead in order to be oversubscribed. So let's break that number down.

1. How many clients do you want per quarter? _____
   Or...

2. How many clients do you want per month? (I only ever assume 10 months of the year will be productive)

_____

Or...

3. How many client intakes do you want per year? _____

Isn't it interesting when you break it down? It feels more empowering to most people to know that their business will be oversubscribed if they can keep up with those targets rather than the endless game of chasing "one more client".

We've just considered some important factors for planning your year of campaigns in advance. We now know who you want to serve, what capacity you have to create a delighted client and when you want to bring them on. We can move to the next step and signal to the market what you're planning and get them to signal back their intention to buy.

CREATE A CAMPAIGN THEME

Every campaign needs to have a theme. It's common for businesses to talk about the seasonal events like Christmas, Valentines and Easter. It's also common to see businesses run campaigns based on price promotions, new product launches or special events. While these can be very effective themes, they often don't set you apart if lots of other businesses are all running with similar messages.

What's impossible to compete with is when your campaigns talk about something bigger than your business.

Chipotle is a Mexican fast food restaurant, but if they talk about Mexican fast food they become commoditized, dull and add to a noisy market place. Instead of talking about burritos and salsa, Chipotle talk about "cultivating a better world".

The food chain has created iconic commercials that address the shortcomings of factory farming and the damage caused by breaking away from traditional food production methods. The ads show famers upset by the way animals are treated and saddened by the chemicals and wastage they are causing. These farmers then decide to go back to their traditional ways and the world is better for it.

The ads barely mention Chipotle and they don't talk about Mexican food at all. These ads have had tens-of-millions of views on YouTube and are shared millions of times on social media; this would have never happened if they talked about their products.

Oversubscribed businesses more often talk about something bigger than what they do. They talk about the lifestyle of their customers, they talk about philosophy, they talk about a big problem they want to solve or they talk about the transformation they want to see in the world.

You must look for the bigger game your business is playing for and beat the drum for it in your campaigns. It's far more compelling for you and for your customers to get involved in a big game than simply focusing on the basic products and services you sell.

In a recent Nike campaign, we see Michael Jordan talking about all his failures. He talks about all the times he failed and how it cost his team the game. He explains that failure is a big part of success. There's no mention of the shoes or the clothes, in fact the Nike brand doesn't appear at all in that commercial (only the "Air Jordan" logo).

Steve Jobs reinvented Apple with the "Think Different" campaign. He championed "misfits and rebels" and reminded us that it's the people who are "crazy enough" who change the world. It was an idea that was much bigger than hard-drives, processor speeds and RAM.

Every business, yours included, is up to something big in the world and you need to be bold enough to share it. It takes courage to stop shouting about your products and to start talking about your big ideas but it's worth it.

The reason you began your business or chose to work on the team you are part of isn't only about the money. You're doing what you do because you believe there's more to it than just the cash. If you can get other people to believe what you believe they will want to be part of what you do too. They key is to talk about something bigger than what you do.

Always chose a campaign theme carefully and execute it masterfully; you can play it safe and revolve your messages around special events, promotions and prices or you can really go for a big win by talking about your bigger picture of the world.

CREATE A CAMPAIGN TIMELINE

When you know the number of campaigns you intend to run, you need to break it down even further into a campaign timeline and divide each campaign into its components:

1 The start date and finish date of each campaign.
2 The communications schedule – emails, direct mail, press releases, advertising, etc.
3 The milestones – price rises, cut-off dates, early bird specials.
4 Supporting events – partnership meetings, pre-launch events, celebrations, sales meetings, etc.
5 Main events – Entertainment, seminars, launch parties, grand opening, etc.
6 Shipping dates – sending out products, delivering the service, etc.
7 Post campaign activity – telling the stories, reporting results, follow up, thank you messages.

All of these components need to be placed on a timeline. It might be monthly for small campaigns or a six-month schedule for bigger ones. My approach is to create campaign timelines on big poster paper or on a large whiteboard. Our team stands around planning in as much detail as we can. We mark in every single email, every meeting, all the webinars, every advertisement, every Facebook post and every sales meeting. When we're done, we take a photo of it and send it to our graphic designer who creates our campaign timeline. We print it out on a poster and put it up on the office wall so that we can mark off each milestone every day.

There's no confusion. We look at the campaign timeline and we do what it says.

Here are a few examples:

A business consultant wants twelve clients a year who would pay $30,000 each for a project. He knows that a perfect client is the owner of a franchise business or a multi-location chain of stores or restaurants. He knows that there are three good times to on board new clients each year. Therefore, he now knows that he needs to create three campaigns a year, each designed to sign on four new clients.

A hair salon knows that it needs 600 clients per year. A perfect client is a busy, young professional male who gets his hair cut every four weeks on average. They already have 350 of these clients, so they are 250 away from being over-subscribed. Every second month they will run a campaign designed to generate 50 new clients.

A large technology provider knows that it will be launching a new product next year and the global head office wants 100,000 units sold in year one. The perfect client would be small business owners, self-employed people with a home office, or students. They decide to create three campaign schedules each focused at the different markets.

A startup business is getting ready to launch, and is seeking to generate 250 users of their beta version website.

They want to get them all in the first few months of launch and then monitor their behaviour for six months. They schedule a beta launch campaign in month one and another campaign in month nine when they plan to expand the user base.

ACTIVITY

Who's your perfect client?

_____

_____

What is your core offering for clients?

_____

_____

What's your product-for-prospects to attract customers?

_____

_____

How many clients will make your business oversubscribed for the year ahead?

_____

_____

How many campaigns will you run in the year ahead? (3–10 is normally the range)

_____

_____

How many clients do you need to generate per campaign?

_____

_____

BUILD UP TO BEING OVERSUBSCRIBED

THE POWER OF SIGNALLING

The Glastonbury Music Festival is considered to be an institution in the music scene. The festival has run for over 30 years and attracts over 120,000 people each year who mostly camp out for the four-day event.

Selling 120,000 tickets sounds like a mammoth task and yet they manage to do it every year in a matter of minutes. They have it down to a fine art and it involves a lot of signalling.

If you are a hopeful attendee the first thing you need to do is signal your interest by pre-registering for tickets. You'll then get an email from the organizers with an overview of the rules and guidelines for buying tickets, as well as the date tickets will go on sale.

They then ask you how many tickets you intend to buy. You log into their website and signal that you will want up to a maximum of six tickets, and they reply that you'll be given a short window of time to buy them on the release date.

A week before release, they name the exact time and date the tickets will be available. They openly share that over 350,000 tickets are pre-registered, but that they'll only issue 120,000. They remind you that all tickets are usually sold in under 30 minutes from the release time. They also inform you that at this point you will not even be told the names of the bands that will be playing – you'll have to buy your tickets "blind".

They tell you that in the months after you buy your ticket they will be releasing the line-up of bands that will be performing at the festival for you. If you're unhappy with the bands, you'll have another window of time to give up your tickets and get a refund. This will also be the small window of time (about 5 minutes) for people who missed out to buy any tickets that were relinquished.

This sounds like an awful lot of trouble, doesn't it? Why can't you just buy a ticket when you want to? Why can't they tell you who the bands are and then you can buy a ticket if you want one? Why can't you get a refund whenever you like? Why can't the organizers stress out all year hoping you buy when you're ready rather than making you follow their plan?

The answer to all of these questions is because the organizers of "Glasto" aren't silly. They know how to stay oversubscribed and signalling is a big part of it.

Signalling is about telling people what's going to happen before it happens. It's about explaining your process and your terms in advance so that the market can prepare itself. It is also about getting your market to signal their intentions back to you before they act, rather than asking people to take action.

Signalling is a big part of getting yourself oversubscribed. Companies that are not oversubscribed don't do much of it, and don't ask their clients to do it either. If they want to sell a new product they simply put a product up for sale on their website or store and hope people buy it.

A Campaign Driven Enterprise won't do that. They will signal their intention to release a new product. They will let people know that there's a limited capacity available and ask their market to signal in kind if they want to know more or buy the product when it's available.

A Campaign Driven Enterprise isn't hoping to sell some products; it's strategically ensuring that the product will be oversubscribed. A big part of becoming oversubscribed involves having the courage to signal your intentions before you act and to name the terms under which you will be doing business in the future.

NAMING YOUR TERMS

Naming your terms sends a powerful signal: "If you want to work with us, you need to behave a certain way."

It takes confidence, too. You'll need to state openly who you want to work with, how many people you can serve and on what terms you'll work with them. When you see a business naming their terms, you know they are on track to be oversubscribed. An oversubscribed restaurant might do things like stating their dress code, their policy on bringing children, or their right to rebook your table if you're not on time.

Is this something they do after they are oversubscribed or something they do in order to become oversubscribed? My belief is that you'll never become oversubscribed if you're not willing to name your terms.

People like to know you have certain standards. They feel reassured that you turn some people away and that you're protective about who's part of your business.

Consider from your own point of view: which business consultant would you rather work with – the one who will work with anyone or the one who insists on interviewing you for an hour before agreeing to take on your business?

Naming your terms isn't about being a snob or only working with the rich. A muddy music festival, a hair-stylist, and a graphic designer can all name their terms. That is what signalling is all about – telling people when something will be made available and how to get it, when they have to register their interest by, when they will have to pay, and on what grounds they will be accepted or rejected. You're setting time limits, performance standards and prerequisites.

Activity

Imagine for a moment that you really didn't "need" people to buy from you. Imagine that you'd secretly won the lottery and your business was only for fun now. What terms would you name in order to ensure business was fun?

_____

_____

_____

Don't ask for the sale – ask for the signal

Most companies market their products for sale. If they have a widget, they run an ad asking people to buy the widget. If they can take on more clients, they run an ad asking people to become a client. But this won't usually result in people rushing in to buy – and it won't leave them oversubscribed.

Rather than asking people to buy, ask them to signal interest. Let them know that there will be a widget for sale soon and if they are interested in more information, can they please email a request or fill in an expression of interest form. This is a much lower commitment for people. Rather than having to get their credit card out right there and then, all they have to do is fill in a form, click "like" or reply to an email.

I've tested this many times and the results always excite me – even when I know what to expect.

When you ask people to buy straight away they only have two choices: they buy or they don't. It's a binary decision. But people aren't binary.

What if someone is 90% ready to buy? They are interested in what you have to offer, would probably purchase if they could just sort out one or two things. If you give them a decision to buy or not to buy, the binary choice forces them to *not* buy. This means hundreds of people might see your offer, be very interested but not 100% ready to buy and you simply don't know that they are interested.

You'll get a better picture if you ask people to signal their interest. A person who is only 25% interested in what you have might still signal their interest to you. Once they've done so, you can make sure they have all the information they need. Or perhaps signalling their interest might prompt them to get the answers they need in order to be 100%.

TRANSPARENCY

One powerful way to boost the impact of your signalling is to add a layer of transparency. This is where you openly show how many people you have sent your signal to and how many have signalled back.

One campaign we ran required people to answer a question on our Facebook forum. Within a day, five times more people answered the question and signalled their interest in our offer than the capacity we had to deliver. Everyone could see that there were five people interested for every unit of capacity we had announced in the email.

The transparency created a level of energy in people. Some said that they felt concerned they would miss out; some put extra effort into their answer and gave reasons why they should be chosen. Some people said they were excited and others said they wouldn't bother getting their hopes up.

When we released the capacity, it was snapped up in a day. People could see how many others had responded on Facebook and they weren't taking chances. They bought the offer as soon as they could.

Apple uses the media to signal and add transparency to their campaigns. When the company releases a new iPhone, they first tell people about it at their iconic

MacWorld conference. CEO Tim Cook will stand up on stage and tell you how remarkable the new features – the battery life, the sensors, the screen, the processor – are going to be.

Then they signal to you the price and the release date, which is normally a few months away. The media goes bananas in the following days and weeks, breaking the story that a new iPhone is coming and instilling in people the fear that they might not be able to get one. They report on Apple's capacity "We are told that the UK will only have 2.5 million units available. You'll have to rush to get one; some people are already camping out."

This doesn't happen by accident. Apple has the world's best PR executives signalling their capacity, their terms and the amount of interest they are getting to the press. They use the world media to add a layer of transparency and it creates palpable energy surrounding a new product launch.

THERE'S ONE OF ME AND LOTS OF YOU

Transparency is a tool whereby you let people see how many other people are indicating their interest to do business with you. It happens when there is a physical line forming out the front door of a restaurant. Or it happens online when people put their names on a list, publicly like a page, or increase the view count of a video or blog.

Transparency is a double-edged sword. It can work for you when you have a lot of people buzzing around your business or against you when you don't. And it is often taking place even if you're not aware of it.

I remember the first time I went to a trade show as an exhibitor. The experience was terrible: person after person turning their nose up at our promotional staff and our brochures. In other environments, people were interested and engaged by what we had to say. But here, most people were withdrawn.

Consider the reason this happens from an attendee's perspective: there are 300 exhibitors who are all trying to get their business. They feel that there's so much choice and it makes them reluctant to engage with any of those choices. So in this situation, transparency was working against us, since it was transparent that we were just one potential option amongst 300 others.

Contrast this with the first promotional workshop event I ran. There were 70 people who were 100% focused on what we had to say. Those people looked around the room and saw one seller and 70 buyers. Transparency was on our side; it was obvious we were oversubscribed.

If you're going to become oversubscribed you need to demonstrate that there's only one of you and plenty of people lining up to take whatever it is you have to offer. If people can see a line forming at your door – physically or metaphorically – they will want to know why and they'll want in.

Avoid scenarios where you appear to be one of many sellers and no one is lining up. This also doesn't mean you don't go to a trade show; you can make it work with the right strategy. I was once a speaker at a trade show and gave a talk at the main stage in the morning. At the end of my talk I told the audience that if they came by our booth and filled in a five-question survey they'd get a free book and some of our samples. All day there was a line-up of people filling in the forms at the booth and it attracted even more people who hadn't seen my talk. We gave them the samples in a brightly coloured bag with our brand on it and somehow it seemed like everyone at the show was walking around with our brand. We used transparency to our advantage.

Keep in mind that being oversubscribed is simply having more people who want your capacity than you have capacity to deliver. If your capacity number is 12, then you become slightly oversubscribed when the 13th person signals interest. If you hit 36 people signalling interest, you're three times oversubscribed; and if people can see that, you'll have a lot of energy built up behind your campaign.

Signalling online causes transparency to go to a whole new level because people can easily see the numbers. In some campaigns I've run, we ask people to signal their intention to do business with us on a Facebook page. We've had posts with hundreds of people saying "I'm in" and "Let me know when I can get one, please."

We've used Twitter hashtags (#) to get people signalling that they are attending our events. Anyone who clicks the hashtag often sees hundreds of people talking about how much they are looking forward to an event. This online transparency adds to the energy buildup you'll need in order to be oversubscribed. Today's world is digital – but if you can master the online world, the real world is your oyster.

THINK MOBILE AND MEDIA FIRST

The first one to five interactions people have with your business are likely to be on their mobile device in the form of media or content. If you email someone, they will probably see it on their phone first. If you tweet to someone they probably see it on their iPhone. If you share a video, a photo, a status update, an event invite or a PDF download, it's probably hitting them on their mobile first. When you think about signalling to your clients or potential clients, it's probably most accurate to picture someone holding their phone.

Of course, they are distracted by other things while they're doing it. Maybe they are in their car, commuting on a train, watching TV, standing on an escalator, watching TV, shopping or with a friend at a coffee shop. They have an infinite number of other things they can skip to if you don't capture their attention. It only takes a split second for them to start reading another tweet, Facebook post, search result, song, map, email, game or movie. This means that if you don't get your signalling right for a mobile device, you probably won't win the business beyond that.

Perhaps this sounds strange to you. Chances are that you used to think of your clients and potential clients sitting at their desk, paying full attention to what they are doing. If they were checking email, they weren't also waiting in line for a coffee. Ten years ago, I made my money by imagining potential clients sitting down reading the daily paper skimming through the headlines, not doing much else. But holding that image in my mind today would be inaccurate and potentially damaging.

Maybe you don't think of yourself as a media or technology business. However, that's a dangerous position to take. No matter what your business is, you are also a media and technology business. It's nearly impossible to become oversubscribed at any scale without the use of media and technology. So if you're not comfortable with it, you'd better hire someone onto your team who is.

Thinking mobile and media means:

- Communicating clearly, concisely and powerfully in bite-sized chunks that link to further content.
- Using images and video that loads fast.
- Producing quality content, images, recordings, video and telling stories.
- Having buttons that work easily on a phone.
- Having a responsive website and blog.
- Having social sharing plugging that work on mobile.
- Giving frequent, bite-sized updates that add value to people.
- Using location relevant content.
- Using context to your advantage.

As Charles Darwin remarked,

> *It is not the most intellectual of the species that survives; it is not the strongest that survives; but the species that survives is the one that is able to adapt to and to adjust best to the changing environment in which it finds itself.*

Thinking "mobile and media first" is key to your survival.

EDUCATE AND ENTERTAIN

So you've signalled your intentions to the market. You've asked them to signal back with their interest. Now you have a captive audience of interested people. Your job is to educate or entertain these people until they are totally comfortable with the idea of buying from you.

Entertainment is a powerful way to do this. It can build rapport, connection and pique emotions. Sport, music, art, food, drinks, humour, introductions, fashion, theatre and the like are your tools for entertaining your guests.

Education is powerful too. It builds trust, understanding and engagement. Trainings, seminars, webinars, workshops, manuals, reports, statistics, thought leadership, guidance, consultation and measurement are all tools for educating your interested people.

EDUCATE   ENTERTAIN

However, combining entertainment and education is potentially dangerous. Trying to do these things at the same time is rarely successful and can go badly if served in the wrong doses. Imagine if they stopped the men's tennis final at Wimbledon to give everyone a tennis lesson. That would be weird.

The best formula is to combine these two using the 80–20 rule. If you're educating people at a workshop, use small amounts of humour in your presentation, serve nice food for lunch and host a few drinks after the workshop in a classy location. Eighty percent education mixed with some light entertainment at the edges. If you're entertaining people at a sporting event, hand out some information kits, have some of your engineers at the event for a few side conversations that happen naturally or follow up with a conversation the week after to answer questions. Eighty percent entertainment with a little bit of education sprinkled around.

Your ultimate goal is to turn people who are interested in working with you from "maybe I would" to "I'd love to". That goal can take time: seven hours, to be specific.

THE 7-HOUR RULE

We met for a business meeting at 2 p.m. and by 9 p.m. that night I knew she was "the one". We'd talked about life, values, the past and the future and I was hit with a new kind of feeling I hadn't had before. As clichéd as it sounds, I was sure I would end up marrying this woman.

It's funny how my story of meeting my wife matches that of many other couples. That sense of "knowing" set in around the first few dates for many people. It's also funny how people tend to make all sorts of big decisions in this same way in a business context.

I've observed that big purchasing decisions will take about seven hours. Whether you are buying a new car, making a career move, engaging a consultant or choosing a holiday destination, when you add up all the time you spend thinking about it, you can be fairly sure it totals about seven hours.

It's also logical that if someone is willing to invest seven hours getting to know about a topic, it's only because they're interested. If they hadn't felt any connection, they wouldn't have hit the seven-hour mark; they would have walked away. During those seven hours, people establish their criteria, look for relevance, develop an emotional connection, build trust, rapport and understanding.

Then something magical happens at about the seven-hour mark. You get sick of thinking about it and you're ready to make a decision.

So how will this help you become oversubscribed?

If you sell something to which a purchaser is required to have an emotional connection, develop trust or gain a new understanding – and if he or she must make a significant decision – you would be silly to try to force the deal to complete sooner than seven hours.

Japanese businessmen know this. They will rarely talk business until after a round of golf or two. It can actually blow the deal to bring up the topic of business too soon.

None of this matters if you are selling something trivial that a person doesn't need to learn about. It also doesn't matter if you're happy to compete purely on price with tiny margins. But when you want to offer something new or important and you want to be fairly rewarded, the seven-hour rule is vital. Expect your interested people to "think about it" for up to seven hours while they explore their options. Also consider whether they would be more likely to choose you if you provided them with seven hours of content, ideas, conversation and connection.

To scale this concept, your goal is to clock up seven hours with as many people as possible using your tools of entertainment and education. You don't want to do this in a creepy, annoying or pestering way. You want people to want to spend seven hours with you. Maybe you host great parties, maybe you chair industry meetings, or maybe you take people out for coffee once a month. As long as people like spending time with you it won't be time wasted.

Two great things happen after you have a seven-hour relationship. Firstly, you don't feel uneasy offering something of value; and secondly, you are less likely to blow the relationship by offering something you don't fully believe in.

BRAINS DON'T KNOW IT'S DIGITAL

Social media and digital technology allow you to leverage this process even more. If people read your blogs, follow your tweets, watch your online videos, listen to your podcast, click through your slides or flick through your photos, it's as good as sitting face to face. Strangely, the human brain can't distinguish between digital media and real life (which is why we still feel sad when a celebrity dies, even though we didn't ever meet them).

In the same way, celebrity endorsements are effective because of the seven-hour rule. You are seeing someone familiar, who you have most likely spent seven hours watching, recommending a product. Companies who use celebrity endorsements are effectively buying lots of 7-hour+ relationships.

One of the reasons I write books is because they go out and build relationships with people at a scale I could never accomplish on my own.

I've seen people tweet "I'm curled up in bed with Daniel Priestley" or "I'm sitting on the beach, enjoying my holiday with Daniel Priestley". Of course, they are just reading my book, but it feels more personal than that.

Google looks at it another way. They call it Zero Moments of Truth (ZMOT), which is another name for various data points that a person might find about you as they are making a purchasing decision. Their research indicates that it takes an average of 11 "ZMOTs" or touches in order to build up trust with someone. They also advocate that a lot of these touch points can be found online as digital content.

You should have 7 hours or 11 touches of relationship-building content at your disposal in your business at any given time. Articles, podcasts, videos, apps, questionnaires, reports, illustrations, books, case studies and events – all of it counts towards hitting the mark.

Try out the seven-hour rule in your own business and see if life gets easier. If you experience what I have, you will find that you don't need to push for sales, you get better joint ventures and partnerships, and you have more fun, too – all by spending quality time with people.

PRODUCTS-FOR-PROSPECTS

As you know by now, your capacity is based upon your ability to deliver a full and remarkable solution to a person who can pay for it at a price that's profitable. Let's call that product or service – whatever it is – your "core offering". If you're BMW, your core offering is cars. If you're Citibank, your core offering is finance. If you're a restaurant, your core offering is food. In short, it's the thing you're most known for and from which you typically make your money.

Selling your core offering is the ultimate goal; but as we discussed, in order to be oversubscribed on that offering you'll need to educate and entertain people for 7 hours or for 11 touches. One way to do that is to create a series of products-for-prospects. These are designed to be given cheaply or freely in order to achieve the goal of educating or entertaining people. A book is a product-for-prospects; an audio podcast is a product-for-prospects; and a software download, a sample, a workshop, a report, a party, tickets to a game, merchandise or apparel could all be products-for-prospects.

If BMW wants to sell more cars, it could advertise cars – or it could advertise a track-day, an exclusive event, a weekend test-drive or BMW accessories. All of these pre-purchases would indicate that a person is interested enough to spend some money or some time invested in the brand. Citibank could sell more mortgages if it created a powerful report, released a book, hosted a series of talks or produced a useful software download.

Your business will sell more of its core offering if you produce more products-for-prospects too. It's a simple activity: your job is to create scalable products that help to educate or entertain your market. Ideally, you also want to create a product-for-prospects that helps you to learn more about your client, too. You might want their contact details or to better understand their needs. An elegant product-for-prospects will achieve those goals.

Consider what it would be like if your capacity was 100 clients per year and you sold 2,500 products for prospects. Consider how you'd feel if you had twenty-five times more people giving you their details and expressing interest than you could even look after as a client.

The good news is you don't need that many to be safely oversubscribed.

RELEASE WHEN OVERSUBSCRIBED

OVERSUBSCRIBE YOUR CAPACITY

You don't release your capacity *until* you are oversubscribed – and, just to review, you become oversubscribed when more people want your capacity than you can deliver it to. In short, you have more buyers than sellers.

If your capacity number is 100, you're slightly oversubscribed at 101. Being slightly oversubscribed isn't good enough though and you probably want to know how many people you need to educate and entertain before you are sufficiently oversubscribed.

Up until this point, you've named your capacity, signalled it to market and then asked people to signal their interest back to you. After that, you've engaged in the process of entertaining and educating people who are interested. After clocking up significant education and entertainment with your potential clients, you have three ways to know when you've hit the point of being sufficiently oversubscribed.

1 **Five times capacity for strongly signalled interest** – this means the number of people who have strongly signalled their interest to you is five times more than the amount of capacity you have. Example: You have capacity to sell 5 products and 25 people have paid a small holding deposit.

2 **Ten times capacity for educated or entertained customers** – this is when the number of perfect clients who have been educated or entertained by you is ten times the capacity. Example: you have capacity for 5 clients and 50 perfect clients have attended an event you ran that educated people about what you can do for them.

3 **One hundred times capacity for soft interest** – Oversubscribe your capacity by a factor of 100:1 if people are only signalling interest softly such as watching videos online, downloading a free report or entering a competition. Example: Your capacity is five clients and you have 500 people who have downloaded a 20-page report from your website.

Exceeding any of these three targets will give you the confidence that you're sufficiently oversubscribed.

If you've not hit any of these targets, you have to continue the process of building up interest by signalling and educating/entertaining until you do. This might mean that you continue to run several more events, sell more products-for-prospects or push for more downloads until you've met one of the three criteria.

MEASURING INTEREST

Knowing that you're oversubscribed is an important part of the process. It can be costly to educate and entertain people and if you do it beyond the point where you need to, you might make yourself broke before you have a chance to sell anything substantial. The guidelines I've given require you to measure two factors:

1. The **quantity** of signalled interest – This could be downloads, competition entries, registrations, tickets, pre-sales, deposits, emails, opt-ins, registrations of interest.
2. The **quality** of the signaled interest – Is it fairly weak interest involving no real commitment; or is it strong interest that signals a real intention to complete the deal?

To measure the quantity of signalled interest you need a central score board. You need to be able to see your score-board quickly and easily as you're running your campaigns to know if you're on or off target.

Some people might email you, some might fill in a form online, and some might put their business card in a goldfish bowl. This might mean you have to collate data from several sources so you can see in one place the various ways people have signalled interest to you. The quality of the signals requires you to make a judgment call about the level of commitment a person has given you in order to send that signal.

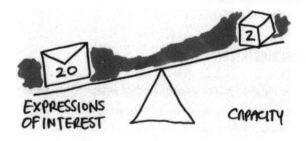

The highest quality signals are pre-payments or deposits. If you pre-register your interest in an exclusive sports car you usually have to put down a deposit and if you're not selected, you'll get the deposit refunded. Close in strength would be a pre-approval process that required someone to submit finance applications or proof of funds. To be strongly oversubscribed you'll need five times more of these strong signals than you have capacity to deliver. A moderate signal would be the purchase of a product-for-prospects, filling in a detailed survey, attending an event for several hours or enrolling in a training program relating to the purchase of your core offering. If you have ten times your capacity in these moderate signals, you could assume you're safely oversubscribed.

A very soft signal would be downloading a document, entering an email address into your website lead-capture form, watching online videos, entering a competition or taking a free sample. These weak signals require one hundred times your capacity in order to comfortably know you're in the zone of being oversubscribed sufficiently.

You'll get a better sense of how strong various signals are as you run more and more campaigns. You might discover that one in six people who email your office asking for your price list ends up buying. You can then run entire campaigns designed to get six times capacity to email your office for a price list.

SELECTION PROCESS

The process up until this point has been a little convoluted for a reason: it's weeded people out, educated people and given you a chance to get to know people. At this point, you get the chance to select *who* you want as your clients. You're able to release the capacity you have to the market and make sure it goes to the people you choose.

The purpose of being oversubscribed is so you can be selective as to who you will work with or sell to. Being selective creates a powerful self-fulfilling prophecy. Oversubscribed businesses usually find that they end up selecting the die-hard fans. And of course, there's a reason they are die-hard fans: they love what you do and find it highly valuable. If they love what you do and are willing to pay for it, there's a good chance they'll be your kind of people too. You'll enjoy working with them and they will rave about the experience.

Conversely, people whose arms you really needed to twist in order to buy will probably cause you trouble. They will have buyer's remorse, might complain about price or value because they aren't quite right. As we've discussed previously, Apple releases its initial capacity of new phones or other products to people who line up at their retail stores. These die-hard fans are the ones who write blogs, pose for the media and generally create the hysteria that others get caught up in. It's no wonder these are the people who Apple selects to get their products first.

MANAGING ENERGY

There's an art to the selection process or the product release – one that allows you to maximize the built-up energy you've created through signalling, entertaining and educating a lot of people. Your goal is to keep energy high for people's desire to buy from you. If you lose that spark, the entire campaign can fall apart and your market loses interest.

We talked at the beginning of the book about the balance of buyers and sellers being the critical factor for building energy and being oversubscribed. We can use several methods to maintain this balance and keep the ratio of buyers and sellers unbalanced so you stay oversubscribed:

1 **Staged release**: We release capacity in smaller chunks.
2 **Special/limited editions:** We break capacity into smaller sub-groups.
3 **Price rises and time limits**: We create a price rise mechanism based on time or volume sales.

It's critical not to use these tools on a whim while you're mid-way through a campaign, as it will come across as tacky and opportunistic. You only want to employ these three techniques if you plan them from the outset. If you put them into your campaign plan, then they are at your disposal.

Let's look at these tools in more detail:

STAGED RELEASE

In November 2013, the original cast of British comedy group Monty Python announced they would be rejoining for one night only to do a stage production at the O2 Arena in London. It was the first time in decades that they had performed together and the media buzzed with enthusiasm. "For one night only," the newscasters chorused, "these comedic geniuses will entertain just a few thousand lucky fans!" This was big news for anyone who loves Monty

Python and many people set an alarm to try and buy a ticket on the day of the release. Sadly, however, unless you bought in the first 40 seconds of tickets going on sale, you missed the boat.

That night on the evening news, sad fans were interviewed and shared how disappointed they were to miss out. "It's just not fair on us real fans who've waited so long for this" one man said sadly to camera. "I wouldn't sell my ticket for £1,000" said a lovely lady who was fortunate enough to have got through in time and snap up a ticket for £32. Many people felt cheated that they wanted something that they simply couldn't buy.

Or so they thought.

The next day, original Python John Cleese proudly announced that the performers and promoters had agreed to do another nine dates, making another 45,000 tickets available for all those unlucky people who missed out.

Once again, the evening news carried the story. "Due to outstanding demand from dedicated Monty Python fans, the cast and crew have agreed to another 10 shows but be warned, tickets previously sold out in 45 seconds flat. If you want a ticket, you better get in early when tickets go on sale tomorrow at 10am."

Sure enough, the following morning my fiancé and I were sat with our fingers hovering over the refresh button to get ourselves a ticket to the show. Up popped two tickets for £149 each that we gladly snapped up. Even when I know what they are doing it still works!

The reality is that it's highly unlikely the promoters and performers of the show could easily book nine more consecutive days at the O2 Arena at short notice. It's actually much more likely that they used a technique called a "staged release" to sell over 150,000 tickets to their show. A staged release is where you only release quantities of your capacity over several stages. You market the first batch or a small "early bird" quantity of your product and then follow up at a later date with additional availability. You'll often see Apple do this by announcing through the press that they have an "initial shipment" of phones that is limited and the future shipments won't arrive until a later date.

SPECIAL EDITIONS

The business team members behind the *Star Wars* franchise are the masters of the universe when it comes to special editions. There have only been six movies made over 35 years, but it seems like there's always a new *Star Wars* special edition available. Box sets, added content, bundles, special merchandise and even special packaging lead to the creation of a special edition.

The Beatles were remarkable musicians and equally impressive marketers. Their team continues to release special editions of the Beatles catalogue. There's the edition with previously unheard studio conversations, the edition that's remastered, the edition of Number 1 songs. Each special edition contains many of the same songs every fan knows. Many editions consist of a "limited run" (which could actually be hundreds of thousands).

How could your business create special editions of what you do too? What kind of offering could include special features, only be for a special group of people or limited in its production?

Consider creating a special version of what you do that is only for a specific demographic. Maybe you do a version only for under-30s, maybe a version that's only for high-net-worth individuals, or one for people who work in the medical industry. Get creative and think through all the ways you could turn what you do into a "special edition".

PRICE RISES AND TIME LIMITS

Amazon has daily book deals. These are genuine reductions in the price of Kindle ebooks that they don't repeat regularly. The first 18 months that my last book *Entrepreneur Revolution* was out, Amazon UK selected it for a promotion for just one day. On that day, my book was priced for £1.90 discounted from the usual £8.90.

I was impressed by how many sold on that day. The book normally sits at #2000 for all books on the site, but for that day it shot up to the top #150 books. People love a genuine bargain. Conversely, I've seen the demise of most daily deal sites because many of the deals aren't genuine. For starters the discount isn't always a real discount. Many say that the product is "normally $39"; however a quick

Google search reveals that it's normally $19 on a dozen different sites.

Secondly, the deal isn't for one day. You can go onto the site and see dozens of deals from previous months and buy the deal for the same price. Consumers aren't dumb; they figure out pretty fast that it's not a "deal" and it's not "daily".

There's only one occasion when a price and time promotion works – when it's a genuine deal for a very short period of time. Price promotions don't work anymore if people can access the deal elsewhere or if the deal lasts for anything more than 24 hours. And you can never underestimate the consumer's ability to figure you out quickly. We live in a time where people have access to enormous amounts of information and they get wise to business tricks.

On the flip side, if you run a real deal promotion that you truly *are* only offering for a very short period of time (less than 24 hours), you can achieve a fantastic result. Look at your business and decide what you'd be willing to radically reduce in price for 24 hours. If it's a product-for-prospects, then it's going to drive your core business anyway, so go for it.

SALES CONVERSATIONS VS. CHIT-CHATS

You've done the work to build up a lot of energy behind your campaign, and the people you're meeting are already pre-sold. Many have clocked up 7 hours online, bought a product-for-prospects, Googled you and read up on your background.

That doesn't mean every one of them is ready to buy; it means they are *pre-sold*. And pre-sold people still require a sales conversation in most cases. They might need to talk to someone, get some questions answered, explore some options or simply be reassured.

What they *don't* need is chit-chat. They aren't interested in talking about the weather or sports for long periods of time; your content and your products have already built enough trust and rapport for the discussion to focus on that.

I see so many struggling businesses whose people pathologically refuse to have a sales conversation. And because they hate asking for the business, they don't get much of it.

A sales conversation is scripted and accompanied by materials like brochures or case studies. A sales conversation follows a predictable pattern – one for which you and your sales people have rehearsed. This means that when the time comes to ask for the business, a sales conversation allows for it to happen naturally. A sales conversation gets the deal done.

Sales conversations are unavoidable. Even when you are oversubscribed with people who know you, like you and trust you, you still need to maximize your results by having sales conversations.

You will get a lot of people buying from you during a successful campaign. This is an indicator that there are a lot more people who are on the fence and just need that quick conversation to assure them. Following up with sales conversations can quadruple the results you get from your campaigns.

You must mop up after your campaigns. All that buzz you created will go to waste if you're not following up with warm leads, booking face-to-face appointments, hitting the phones and making sure payments are made.

In every campaign I've ever run, the sales follow up turned it from a break-even campaign to a highly profitable campaign.

To be clear:

- Sales conversations are scripted; chit-chat isn't.
- Sales conversations have brochures and materials present; chit-chat doesn't.
- Sales conversations ask for the business; chit-chat leaves it open-ended.
- Sales conversations result in an order form filled out or detailed database notes logged on the CRM; chit-chats are forgotten.
- Sales conversations make your business work; chit-chat doesn't.

Google, Ferrari, Rolex, Coke, IBM and Virgin all have trained sales people who have sales conversations. If the biggest brands in the world are doing this, your business is going to need you and your team to be trained up in sales too.

Being oversubscribed and running powerful campaigns doesn't *remove* the need to sell. It gives you more opportunities to sell and better qualified people to sell to.

SET YOUR TARGETS AND STAY FIRM

When you get a rush of people who all want to buy from you and you know your capacity is going to become over-subscribed, there's always the temptation to raise your prices on the spot or to expand your capacity numbers.

I want to urge you not to do it. It's more important that you stay oversubscribed and that you can be trusted at your word rather than being opportunistic. If you name a price, stick to that price. Only move the price if you said you would from the beginning or after a campaign is completely finished and you're now in a position to rename the price.

There's also a good chance that if your price worked, you shouldn't mess with it too much. Walmart got themselves deeply oversubscribed by offering low prices. They stayed oversubscribed for decades and grew one of the world's most financially successful businesses because they kept prices low.

Imagine if Sam Walton had bumped his prices up each month and moved away from his winning formula. After a few years, the crowds would stop coming and the business would stop expanding. Sam knew that his winning formula was "stack it high, sell it cheap". Price was his strategy for staying oversubscribed.

It might turn out that you become oversubscribed because of price too. Maybe your winning formula is that you offer more value for less money. If that's the case, you might just become a commodity if you mess with the price too much.

Never underestimate the powerful appeal of a bargain price – for the mass market the lure of price is intoxicating. People will drive an hour, line up and jostle with other shoppers for a genuine discount. If you figure out a way to keep prices low and still make a decent profit, don't get greedy; use it as part of your winning formula. Keep the price low and make sure people are lining up for it.

Likewise, you shouldn't shift your available capacity up either. If what you're doing is working there's a strong desire to increase your capacity numbers to meet the demand and make money fast. You might hear yourself say *"Did I say I could only accept 12 clients this year? Oops – I meant to say 20."*

It's not easy turning people away – but it's worth it for several reasons:

1 **Saying yes when you can't deliver sets you up to fail.** After accepting more customers than you can handle, you figure that you'll surely find a way to look after them – somehow. You'll hire more staff, buy new equipment, or outsource to a third party supplier. But those

things still take up your time and take you away from the care and attention you'd planned on giving to your clients. By exceeding your capacity, you run the risk of letting down each and every one of your clients – not just the extra few.

2 **People will learn not to take you at your word.** If you go over your capacity, people will eventually find out and will assume everything you say is nothing more than a gimmick. They will assume your special price is the normal price, your limited-time offer is available all the time and your exclusive deal is for anyone. When you stick to your guns, people learn that you mean business – and if they want to access your products and services, they'd better take action when you ask them to.

3 **Every person you turn away is a walking advertisement for your brand.** Have you considered that people very rarely get turned away from spending money and they will probably tell quite a few friends when it happens to them? They will say, "I tried to pay more, I begged, I negotiated and pleaded but they didn't budge and refused to take my money!" That story gets around and your business becomes known for it.

Sticking to your price and your capacity is an important part of the CDE (Campaign Driven Enterprise) Method. It's these rigid numbers that create attraction for you in the long term. You might miss out on a quick sale but you'll keep business on the boil for longer if you're willing to hold steady.

REMARKABLE DELIVERY

POSITIVELY REMARKABLE DELIVERY

This is the most important step in the process by far. The old adage of "Sell the sizzle not the steak" is over. We live in a world whereby if the "steak" is no good, the business is over.

People talk. Prior to social media, a dissatisfied customer told 11 people according to research. Today a dissatisfied customer might have 1,000 friends on Facebook, several hundred Twitter followers and their negative review of your business could become indexed on Google and haunt you for years.

Conversely, if people see your business as remarkable for positive reasons, all of these factors begin working in your favour. If people love what you do, they can tell thousands of people.

The payoff for being remarkable is immense; for one thing, it reduces your marketing costs to zero. There were no marketing costs for Benedict Cumberbatch's Hamlet. He's such a remarkable actor that his shows sold out in world record speed. Remarkable delivery creates attraction with velocity and no amount of marketing expense will carry the load for a poor performance these days. Today, your job is to "cook great steak" and let your customers create the "sizzle" for you. Your marketing team is comprised of your clients, and your long-term lead generation strategy is being brilliant.

We've talked a lot about promotional activity that builds up energy. Along with this comes an expectation. If you don't meet that expectation, you're running a huge risk. The word "remarkable" means "worthy of being talked about". In order to build your business, you need almost all of your clients to talk about you in a positive way.

The real test for your business to pass is whether it is worthy of being talked about. Will people speak positively about you after they have purchased? Will they share your story? Will they recommend you to their friends? Would a customer link to your blog from their website? Is your brochure worth passing on to a friend? Is your service worth tweeting about? Would I take a photo of your product and upload it on Facebook? Would someone make a YouTube video about how wonderfully your staff treated them? Would your staff tell their friends they should work for your company? Would a competitor say they want to be like you? Would the newspapers write a positive story about you?

If you're answering yes to all these questions, you're positively remarkable.

Don't just think about one aspect of your business; the whole lot has to be positively remarkable if you're going to stay oversubscribed long term.

THE REMARKABLE AUDIT

Look at every touchpoint in your business – your website, brochures, people, products, premises, ads, staff handbook, uniforms, packaging – and ask yourself the question, "Is this touchpoint positively remarkable?" You can list off every touchpoint in a spreadsheet, not only for the customers but also for the team and the suppliers too. Every person who touches your business should find it remarkable.

As your scrutinize point-by-point, score yourself on a scale of 1–10 to determine where your organization is right now. It might be disheartening at first when you see how much work there is to be done in order to have a remarkable enterprise.

Don't be discouraged. Your business has come this far on these terms. Imagine how far it will go when you've improved a few more of the touchpoints to the level of 10 out of 10 for being "positively remarkable".

Identify one or two things a month to improve and invest in them. The secret to creating a great business is to invest into remarkable delivery. The world's fastest growing companies are spending 5–15% of their revenues on research, development, innovation and training. They're not spending it on marketing campaigns like they used to, they're spending on making what they deliver positively remarkable.

The best product wins. If you commit to build the best product and keep investing in it, you're playing a winning strategy. If you surround that product with remarkable touchpoints, you'll be unstoppable.

Embrace the challenge. Lean into the discomfort of how much there is still to be done. That discomfort is your friend; it's keeping the "wannabes" and posers out of your league. Embrace the complexity of business. If it were easy, everyone would be doing it; if it were simple, there wouldn't be any payoff. If creating value were straightforward, it wouldn't be valuable.

ENERGY UP, DOWN OR SIDEWAYS

I went to see magicians "Penn & Teller" for their UK tour in London a few years ago. Having grown up watching their TV programmes and hearing about their Las Vegas shows, my expectations were high.

The show was everything I expected. They were funny, witty, irreverent and highly skilful in delivering their magic tricks. I enjoyed the show, it was as great as I had expected. But what happened as I walked out of the theatre *totally* blew me away.

I saw a crowd of people forming in two big circles on the pavement out the front. In the middle of the circles stood Penn and Teller delivering their street magic performance with the crowd. They posed for photos, made objects disappear, and had the crowd in historical laughter. It was the highlight of the evening for anyone who stuck around.

They didn't *need* to do this. Everyone had enjoyed the show. Everyone was satisfied. Everyone had got what they paid for. But that wasn't enough for these consummate entertainers; they had to leave people with more than they expected.

People are emotional creatures – even the ones who claim not to be. Emotions drive loyalty, trust, connection and ultimately purchasing decisions more than anything else. Emotions cause businesses to become oversubscribed. Emotions are little storms of energy that happen in the bodies and minds of your customers, clients, team members and suppliers. And we can categorize this energy in three ways: up, down or sideways.

- **Up** energy comes from delight, love, spontaneous joy, pleasant surprise, magic and unexpected caring. It's caused from positive experiences that you weren't expecting.
- **Down** energy comes from dissatisfaction, disappointment, anger, annoyance, outrage and resentment. It comes from negative experiences that weren't communicated in advance.
- **Sideways** energy comes from satisfaction, indifference or an exchange. It's the result of a job well done as you would expect.

Only when you leave people "uplifted" will they talk about you in a positive way. If you leave them satisfied (sideways energy) they won't talk about you and all your efforts that went into satisfying them will have been for nothing. If you leave people on a downer, your business will suffer as people talk about the emotions that come from down energy.

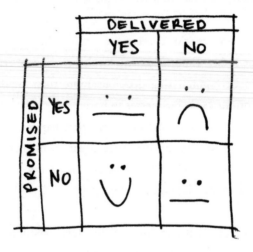

There's a simple principle when it comes to leaving people uplifted: do something great that people didn't see coming. If you buy a Porsche that is supposed to arrive in three days, you'll be pleased if it arrives on time and disappointed if it comes on day four. Strangely, if you're told that it won't be ready for six weeks and then they deliver it in four weeks, you'll be ecstatic.

If a company says to you "sorry we messed up, we will send you some flowers as an apology", you won't feel much emotion when they arrive. If the flowers arrive unexpectedly, you'll be blown away.

The key to leaving people uplifted is to keep quiet about some of the good stuff you know you can deliver. Don't talk about it, keep your mouth shut, and leave it as a surprise.

Had Penn & Teller told people that their ticket included a street magic performance after the theatre show, no one would have thought it was amazing because they would have been expecting it. In fact, some people would have felt annoyed that they didn't get a good spot outside and couldn't hear the jokes properly.

When you sell, only talk about 70% of what you intend on doing. When you make a promise, dial it back a little so that the delivery of that promise is better than what was expected. Keep some magic up your sleeve.

FROM NOW ON, YOU'RE ALSO AN IT BUSINESS

In the times we live in, "We're not very techie" is the sound businesses make before they die.

I don't care if you're running a bakery, a hair salon, a consulting service or a training company; whatever you do, you're also in the technology business. It's simply not possible to deliver a remarkable experience to your customers without the help of technology these days.

You need a system that keeps track of all your client interactions, one that manages delivery of your products, one for setting follow-up reminders and notifications. Without this automation, you can't scale remarkable delivery. And even if you aren't particularly tech savvy, someone on your team needs to be. To be effective as a Campaign Driven Enterprise your business will need to be fast at building web pages, collecting meaningful data, powerfully using that data and optimizing your business online. If you're going to run campaigns and become oversubscribed, you need to know what's worth paying for, what's worth doing in-house and what you can bolt together for free.

It shocks me to discover how many entrepreneurs are completely unaware that they are still paying £2,000+ for something that is now available for under £100. And beyond that, it amazes me how many businesses have seven staff when they could get away with five and a simple piece of software. Effectively they are paying $80,000 too much each year to perform a basic service. They could be using that money to grow the business and hire more of the right people.

FILING CABINETS   CLOUD

At the very least, find a technology supplier who you can work closely with. Since 2007 we've used So Technology (www.sotechnology.co.uk) as our cornerstone technology partner. The team there now knows our business and can pull together a new promotional landing page quickly and powerfully. When we have a new idea, we can execute it in days – not weeks.

I'm always shocked when I can't find a YouTube video, a blog or a Twitter feed for a business. I'm concerned when I see a standard "brochure website" for a business and there's clearly not been innovation there for years. The things that are possible in today's technology driven world are mind bending. The level of sophistication you can build into your marketing and delivery systems is extraordinary – and not terribly expensive.

It's not 2012 anymore. There are no excuses. If you want to grow, a big part of your business is technology.

CELEBRATE AND INNOVATE

STORIES, NUMBERS AND INSIGHTS

The final phase of this process is to celebrate and innovate.

Celebration and innovations are about *publicly sharing* the success of your campaigns, rewarding the people who made it all possible and looking for ways to make it better next time. There's always a temptation after a campaign to roll up your sleeves and do another one. It's quite addictive when you experience the buzz of a campaign and end up oversubscribed.

But if you do that, you'll have missed a crucial step. You'll repeat mistakes and have failed to retain valuable assets.

Instead of rushing straight into the next campaign, you must complete this final phase. You need to hunt down the stories, capture the numbers, interrogate the data – then learn, share, congratulate and reward those involved. You need stories, numbers and insights. Celebration and innovation is about capturing them and using them powerfully.

TELL YOUR STORIES

Creating an expensive men's watch is simple – there are two main ingredients. First, locate your company in Switzerland. Second, begin making watches at least 100 years ago.

If you have those two things, you'll be well on your way to charging a small fortune for a timepiece that every man aspires to own. Rolex, Omega, Breitling, IWC, Jaeger-LeCoultre, Zenith, Tag Heuer, and Longines all follow this formula successfully.

Then there's Bremont, a British company founded as recently as 2002 and who are unable to keep up with the demand for their limited range of chronographs. They aren't Swiss, they only recently celebrated their 10th birthday – yet they have taken a leading position in the fiercely competitive luxury watch business.

They've been able to do this because people don't buy watches because of the geography or the age of the maker. People buy watches because of the story each watch tells.

According to Bremont co-founder Giles English, "Under a critic's scrutiny, every watch we make has to be of the highest quality. Separate from the brand and our story, the product has to stand rigour; however, we know the reason people buy our watches is because of the emotion and the passion that comes through in our story."

Bremont is remarkable at telling those stories and it all begins with the founding of the company, a story about two brothers who share the love of flying with their charismatic father. Then the tragic story of losing their dad in a light aircraft accident, which led to the story of the impassioned decision to fulfil an ambition and create a company making pilots' watches. There's a delightful story about the way the company got its name after the brothers performed an unplanned landing on a flying adventure.

Immediately you feel a sense of connection; when you hear their story, you almost feel part of it.

Each watch these brothers make has a story too. There's the range that was inspired by a B-2 stealth bomber pilot who wanted a completely black watch to match his completely black jet. There's the story of how they are the only company to test their watches for supersonic ejector seat deployment from a fighter plane. There's the story about how every pilot who ejects (and survives) gets a special red bezel fitted to their watch. There are stories about adventurers who take Bremont watches to the Arctic, to the depths of the oceans, to the deserts, to the upper atmosphere and deep into remote jungles.

They have watches that you can *only* buy if you are "pre-authorized military personnel". There's a timepiece that's hand painted by Ronnie Wood of the Rolling Stones. A watch created for Scotland Yard detectives and another for a Hollywood movie about the Secret Service. There's the story they tell about how each glass face is coated with

9 layers of anti-scratch protectant. How they have a special way of making their steel stronger than . . . well, steel.

Before this company releases a watch they first start telling its story. There's a watch that contains parts from a significant WWII plane. There's a watch that contains parts from Bletchley Park's code-breaking equipment and the watch that will raise money to preserve an historical sight.

As a result of telling these stories, many of the watches are sold out on the week they are released.

These stories are crucial. They are as much a part of the product as the movement contained within the casing. Combined with a high-quality product, these stories translate into a business that is constantly oversubscribed. In fact, some of Bremont's used watches sell for triple what they cost new!

There's a lesson here for any company that wants to punch above its weight and stay oversubscribed: *tell your stories*.

The truth is, most people who buy a Bremont watch aren't going to fly a B-2 stealth bomber or eject from a supersonic jet. Most of their customers won't go to the Arctic, set a new free diving record or spend a week alone in the Amazon jungle – and even if they did, many people wouldn't be wearing an expensive, collectable watch while enduring such challenges!

People simply love the romance, the history and the adventure Bremont is sharing with them.

Larger corporate watch brands have hundreds of years' worth of great stories to tell, yet they often run the same boring full page ads you see in any men's magazine. An enlarged watch face, maybe a celebrity or a sportsperson, maybe a picture of a racing car, maybe a few words about being Swiss and founded in 1850-something.

Bremont makes great watches, there's no doubt. But if that was all they did, they wouldn't stand out from their rivals. Bremont is a credible contender to these 100-year-old brands because it's better than them at sharing the stories that unfold while they are making great watches.

In the world of business, many people become so close to their own story that the excitement fades and they stop telling people. They simply take their story for granted.

As you think about your own business, consider how many of your customers know the circumstances that caused you to start your business. How many of your products have a narrative about what makes them unique? How many of your employees can tell you why the company chose its name?

If you're not yet oversubscribed, you might not be telling enough stories.

SO MANY GREAT HIDDEN STORIES

Great, memorable stories don't need to be massive, block-buster tales in order to be powerful; they simply need to be authentic and human.

Small moments of triumph create great stories. Seeing people achieve a personal victory or hit onto a real emotion generates more interest than some huge story that doesn't connect with the heart.

Your job is to drill deep into a story, to find the background, to ask what impact the story has in the future and to examine the finer details. Your job is to capture it in writing, on video or audio and then to make it available online. When you go looking, you'll discover your business is full of stories.

Every restaurant has dozens of stories unfolding on any night. People on a date, people recovering from an illness, people catching up with a loved one. Every accounting practice has access to dozens of touching stories. Their clients are taking risks, building family businesses, employing their first staff member, or raising life-changing investment.

Your business has a story too. There's the story about why it launched and the people involved. There's the story about the tough times it had to endure. There's the story about how a dedicated employee was rewarded. There's the friendship that grew from a professional client relationship. These are special; tell those stories.

THE TRUTH IS IN THE RESULTS

Does a newspaper ad work if you run it upside down? No, it doesn't; and it's a disastrously bad idea. I know that because I measured it.

During a massive campaign in 2005, we ran a lot of ads in dozens of different newspapers. Each ad had a "booking code" next to the phone number and we had our team collect the codes from every person who responded to our ads.

Within months, we had tons of useful data. We knew that ads on an odd page number outperformed ads on an even page number and it was worth paying extra for them. We knew it was no different to have full-colour ads or two-colour ads. But we knew two-colour ads outperformed black-and-white ads.

One day we decided to test what would happen if an ad was run upside down. We wanted to see if people would turn the paper around and if doing so would get a better response. It didn't; in fact, the response rate for the upside down ad fell off a cliff. We only tried it once.

Numbers are powerful. Only when you examine the numbers will you see past the noise. You'll notice what's working and what's not working. So much of business is about conversations – but the numbers add a sobering element.

My business partners and I have a saying around the office: "The truth is in the results." Even if we think we have a great idea but it bombs on the numbers, the truth is we didn't have such a great idea. For that reason we measure everything we can when we're running campaigns.

We measure the cost per lead, the cost per sale, the number of enquiries, the number of people who unsubscribe, the number of clicks, the percentage of conversions. We test one brochure against another. We test long sales conversations against short ones. If we can measure it, we measure it.

Most of the time, we don't do a lot with the data while a campaign is still running. We keep track of it and keep an eye out for basic insights but we're focused on executing our plan as best we can during a campaign. The time to investigate is *after* the campaign. That's when we pour over the data and look for insights, look for ways to improve and to learn the "truth in the results".

The more insights you can take forward into the next campaign the faster you will grow. You'll strip out the wastage, you'll put more energy behind a winning strategy and you'll feel more confident.

THE DEBRIEF

After we've finished an event or an important campaign day, we pull up a circle of chairs and we debrief. We do this while the events of the day are fresh in our minds.

Everyone in the circle gets a say – volunteers, staff, directors, guest speakers and suppliers. If you're there, you'll get asked to join the circle. We go around and have people answer five questions:

1   What would you score our team performance on a scale from 1 to 10 and why?
2   What do you think we did well?

3 What could we have done better?

4 What was a magic moment you noticed?

5 Anything else?

This debrief session helps to complete that important event and to capture insights for the future. Our debrief sessions have led to all sorts of improvements, and are as important to the process as any other part of the campaign. Repeating mistakes is a recipe for disaster.

TIME TO PARTY AND REST

Campaign rollouts can be exhausting mentally, emotionally and physically. They can involve long days, stress, tight deadlines, time-consuming logistics and a lot of moving pieces. It's easy to burn out yourself and your team with a big campaign. We once ran three massive events back to back over a three-month period and made millions in sales. Everything was a huge success – except the entire team was completely shattered. The week after the whole thing was over, three important people resigned. It caused a real dip in morale and a big hole in the company.

We learned a valuable lesson: if you're going to run big campaigns, everyone needs something to look forward to – a party and some downtime. Both of these are important ingredients. At the end of a campaign, regardless of the result, take time to party as a team and recognize the effort that went into the campaign. Some parties will be to celebrate a huge win; some will celebrate the fact you all survived!

Even if you're a small team, find a way to celebrate over a nice dinner and a few bottles of bubbly. After the party, make it a rule that you and your team have scheduled downtime. Even if it's just for a few days, you need to make sure that everyone has an opportunity to switch off – no email, no phone calls, no thinking about work.

The temptation will be to keep working. There are opportunities in your inbox, orders that need to be filled, and calls to return. Forget all of that for a long weekend and go get some fresh air. I promise you that you'll be putting your business at risk if you and your team don't take some time off.

PART III

You, Your Team and the Crazy Times We Live In

IT'S TIME TO PADDLE

A big wave is about to break and if you paddle you can surf it for years to come. If you don't, you'll be swept out to sea.

The wave is a phenomenon called "convergent disruption". It happens when lots of new technology is hitting the market at the same time and suddenly people discover how it all fits together. For the last ten years we've been talking about how technology and the "digital age" have changed everything. But now it's about to get *very* real.

Right now the world of business is having breakthroughs in speech recognition, automation, robotics, logistics, processing power, data management and collaborative sharing of resources. A tipping point has hit when it comes to outsourcing, social media marketing and systemization.

What this all means is that the value of "functional people" is sliding off a cliff. People with respectable jobs in IT, consulting, design, senior management, health care and other professional services are about to see the value of their time diminish substantially.

At the same time the "vital people" who organize things, act as industry spokespeople, are well connected and well known will increase in their value. A lot of very smart people have now figured this out. The writing is on the wall and we're all now working towards this goal.

So here's the key point: every day you spend in your office doing functional things is a day you slip behind in terms of your real value.

On the flip side, every day you are out building your network, connecting with thought leaders, positioning yourself as a key person of influence in your industry is a day that your value is on the rise.

You must do your best in this critical moment to stay on the "surfing" side of the big wave of change. Every campaign you run, every idea you implement, every remarkable product you create and sell, every partnership you forge is you paddling hard.

Merely working hard isn't enough, especially if the work you are doing is functional, replaceable, average, and unremarkable. You need to be creating, storytelling, leading, team building, partnering, deal making, innovating, refining, investing and systemizing what you do. You need to be entrepreneurial.

You can choose the game you want to play – an old game whose rules no longer work for many people, or a new game with new rules and live however you like.

Let's take a look at three games you could choose to play.

STRUGGLE, LIFESTYLE OR PERFORMANCE?

I have interviewed over 3,000 entrepreneurs around the world. I've discovered there are three types of entrepreneurs and leaders who are playing different games in business:

1 **A struggle game:** These people are clinging to the past, getting stuck in fear, refusing to move on and repeating processes that don't work. Businesses or people that are addicted to the struggle, miss the bigger picture because they are too busy working a plan that is predictably set to fail in the future.

   Maybe they were successful in the past and they just can't let go of what once worked for them. Maybe they are fearful about the future and they think not changing feels safer than embracing the times we are in. Maybe they try to do everything on their own and end up being busy rather than productive.

The struggling business owner doesn't become over-subscribed. They just keep doing the stuff that keeps them struggling. They fantasize about some big breakthrough happening to them rather than getting on with creating the breakthrough. Even when you give them answers, they often seem to stay with the struggle because that's the game with which they are most familiar.

It almost doesn't matter why these people are stuck in the struggle. The most important thing is to recognize it's a struggle and to stop repeating things that don't produce the result.

2 **A lifestyle game:** People who are playing the lifestyle game work three to four enjoyable days a week. They are part of a team of three to ten people, run a profitable business, earn a personally healthy income and are passionate about what they do. Some of these people can work from anywhere in the world, and they often do.

These businesses and people have seen and embraced that we are living in special times. They know they don't need to be "factory workers" (neither white collar nor blue collar). They can make money, have fun, travel and deliver great value to others.

The lifestyle business uses the Campaign Driven Enterprise method to generate all the clients they want in a short space of time. They often run 2–4 campaigns per year and enjoy downtime in between.

3 **A high-performance game:** These people live and breathe high performance. They are willing to work

50+ hours a week, amass a team of 50+ people, build their business on a bold mission and a big purpose – and they earn big money.

These people have also figured out that we are in exciting times and they want to change their lives, their families' lives, and impact a lot of people. To continue the surfing metaphor, the lifestyle seeker enjoys surfing the fun, smaller waves on a sunny day; the high-performer is heading out in the storm to catch the really big waves.

A high performer uses the Campaign Driven Enterprise method to fill their capacity fast and then reinvest their energy into raising the capacity. They want to be able to impact as many people as they can and they view the Campaign Driven Enterprise method as a faster way to get there.

LIFESTYLE FIRST THEN PERFORMANCE

I discovered that the vast majority of businesses with which I spoke hadn't achieved a lifestyle business yet, but many people were worrying about how to get to high performance. They hadn't run any successful campaigns and they weren't oversubscribed on a small capacity. Yet they were telling me they wanted to make millions more in sales.

I noticed, however, that most people who achieved high performance had previously hit the lifestyle level. They ran successful campaigns, became oversubscribed, achieved a quality of lifestyle then decided to build a business around a passion to have a bigger impact.

In the same way a person isn't going to get to the top of Mount Everest if they can't get to base camp, it's unlikely you'll get a high performance business if you can't achieve a lifestyle one. If you're not at the lifestyle level and you're not at the high performance level, then you're caught in a struggle. I know that might be hard to hear but it's worth exploring.

The good news is that there is a solution: get your lifestyle in order. Don't even worry about high performance until you've hit a quality of lifestyle and you get bored with it. Run two to four campaigns a year, focus on getting oversubscribed on your capacity and earning good money without working crazy hours.

Break out of your old habits, attend some workshops, work with some mentors and spend time around some people who have the results you want. Let go of the old ideas you're clinging onto and get curious about how you could further embrace the times we are in. Become accustomed to using systems, technology and teams to achieve a lot. Learn to surf on some smaller waves, to have fun again – and then worry about high performance.

Most importantly, surround yourself with other people who want to surf those waves too – and who are also using the Campaign Driven Enterprise method. When you've been surfing for the fun of it for a while and you want to go big, then you can expand the capacity, run bigger campaigns, more often.

Consider that many people fail trying to go from lifestyle to performance for the following reasons.

- Not all businesses are meant to be bigger than a lifestyle business. Some campaigns work twice a year but not ten times a year.
- Not all people are suited for a high performance business. Some people don't like the stress of oversubscribing a large capacity.
- The winning strategies that got you to your lifestyle won't necessarily get you into performance (this can require more funding, bigger deals, more people, and more strategic legal and accounting requirements).

A lifestyle business might make you happy and a performance business might drive you insane. It's like a person who likes playing club level tennis thinking they would enjoy playing professionally – chances are they may not want to practise so much and take bigger risks financially in order to get all the way to Wimbledon.

Your goal is to be oversubscribed, not necessarily to be *big*. Use the methods to find the balance that's right for you.

Both lifestyle and performance businesses require you to work with others – a surefire way to struggle is to try and do everything on your own. Whether you're building a lifestyle business with four people or high-performance business of

150, you'll need a team of talented people around you to implement ideas with you. You'll need mentors to guide you and a peer group that inspires you. As such, this next section of the book focuses on the importance of you and your team showing up to play full out every single day that you show up.

THE CDE TEAM

In order to become oversubscribed, you're going to need to assemble a core group of people to take on the challenge of making your business remarkable and oversubscribed for lifestyle or for high performance. This will require a CDE Team of four people taking on these key roles:

1. **Key Person of Influence:** This is someone who is known, liked and trusted in the industry. They have a powerful network, can make a deal come to fruition, have genuine insights and are commercially successful.
2. **Head of sales and marketing:** This person is responsible for generating warm leads, making sales and collecting referrals.
3. **Head of operations and product:** This person is responsible for delighting customers. The individual in this role is aiming for every client to love their experience so much that they refer more clients to the business.

4 **Head of finance, logistics and reporting:** This person is on top of the money and the numbers. They are looking for ways to create efficiencies, provide useful reports to the team and ensure all compliance issues are handled. They are also responsible for purchasing, logistics and payments.

If you're a small startup hoping to make a splash or working in a large company charged with producing a dynamic result within your division, this little team is a powerful place to start.

Most people think I must have begun as a sole trader, as someone who launched several successful businesses, but the truth is I've never spent a day in business on my own. Every company I've ever started began with a small team covering these four roles from day one.

WHEN TO RECRUIT YOUR TEAM

Imagine you're off to play a game of football. You understand that it's ultimately a team sport and teams will outperform individuals but you decide to start off alone anyway. You reason that if you run onto the field by yourself and start playing, it will be easier and faster than finding a team. You decide to try and kick a few goals on your own and then after you score some points you'll run off and recruit new players for your team.

Clearly, this plan isn't going to work. You're going to get beaten by the opposing teams. They are faster and better organized and each player is focused on their specialized role. Then, you'll become so exhausted running around doing everything alone and there'll be no time to talk to people about joining your team. You won't be scoring goals but the clock will still be ticking.

It's obvious that no one in their right mind would take this approach to a sport. Yet most people miss this logic and think it's entirely appropriate when building their business. They start a project alone, think they will win some clients by themselves and then hire a team when the money is rolling in. But it doesn't work that way. You get exhausted, fall behind, and you lose business to a team that has been assembled from the start.

You must have a high performance team at the beginning of any new project. If you've not done this, then the time to recruit your team is now.

Many bigger businesses even assume that it's ideal to "grow first then recruit", but the team you have has gotten you this far; to go further, you need more and better players.

CREATING CULTURE FROM THE BEGINNING

To create a high performing team, you need a high performance culture. For a small team, culture is about setting a standard for performance and a way of interacting that brings out the desired results.

I begin my team discussions by talking about our seven internal maxims for high performance.

1 **You get what you pitch for and you're always pitching:** Words have power. You can speak into existence almost any outcome. Be careful what you talk about, because you could be "pitching into existence".

2 **Influence comes from output:** Influence isn't something that comes from being cool or using manipulative techniques; rather, it comes from prolific output at a high standard.

3 **Income follows assets:** Assets are anything that would be valuable tomorrow if the team was hit by a bus today. A brochure, a system, a video, a training document and a sales script are all examples of assets. Your job is to create assets and then utilize them to their fullest.

4 **Get famous for the results of your clients:** You aren't trying to put yourselves in the spotlight; instead, you're looking for ways to showcase your clients' success stories and let your results speak for you.

5 **You are in partnership with everyone who touches the business:** Act out of a deep care and respect for the

needs and wants of the people with whom your business comes into contact. Think of everyone as a partner in your success and you as a partner in *their* success.

6 **Prolific beats perfect**: No company is perfect; everyone makes mistakes. Keep moving forward and keep making your business better. Directionally accurate decisions are better than procrastination.

7 **Innovation never ends**: Top companies spend 5–15% of their revenues on research, training and development. Stagnant companies avoid innovation, training, development and research because of what they perceive it costs. You invest in innovation and it doesn't stop.

These seven maxims set a tone and help to plant the seeds of a high performance culture. Feel free to borrow them.

THE ROLES OF A CORE CDE TEAM

The entire CDE Team has one main goal: to become over-subscribed. Together the team will work, innovate, adapt and persevere until they meet and maintain that goal.

Let's explore each team member's role in more detail:

ROLE 1: THE "KEY PERSON OF INFLUENCE"

Every project needs a Key Person of Influence driving it – a leader who's bringing it all together. As discussed previously, this person needs to be known, liked and trusted within their industry so they can get buy-in from all the other key people who can make a project succeed.

The Key Person of Influence needs to be able to sell the vision. They must get the message right and assemble the stakeholders and the team. They need to make the ultimate decisions with the support of their team.

Five core strengths make someone a Key Person of Influence, and like any other skills, anyone can learn and develop these strengths:

1 **Pitching**: The ability to clearly communicate your message in a way that influences people to become involved in your projects. You'll need pitching skills to get your team together, and to procure funding, partners and sales.
2 **Publishing**: The ability to write compelling blogs, articles, reports and content that people can read, relate to and share with others. Being oversubscribed requires you to spread a message, and today that means the message needs to be in print *and* online.
3 **Productizing**: The ability to turn valuable insights into products (or "productized service-offerings") that can scale. Hot products are at the centre of every oversubscribed business.
4 **Profile**: The ability to take ideas "above the noise" and to gain visibility for yourself and your cause. It also means that this Key Person of Influence has an existing profile that they can leverage.

5 **Partnerships**: The ability to form strategic alliances with other valuable people who can make things happen faster.

Nothing really gets done without a Key Person of Influence. You can have systems and products and ideas and resources but it will all sit dormant without a driving force behind it.

Are you willing to be that person? Will you lead the team? Will you put your head above the parapet? If not you, then who? The project needs someone to do this and it's not optional or an "extra".

When I started my first business, I was a 22-year-old with no track record. I found an elder statesman of my industry and paid him a percentage of every sale to be the Key Person of Influence for my business. Although this man had retired, simply having his name attached to our business was enough to open the doors we needed opened. It was also highly valuable to have his discerning eye on some of our bigger decisions.

You can't achieve success without a Key Person of Influence involved *somewhere*. It just doesn't happen. And if you don't feel ready to play this role yourself, then you need to get someone with influence to do so. You must position yourself as a Key Person of Influence and work alongside other key people of influence in order to become oversubscribed.

These days, there are three layers of branding your business needs in order to really take off:

Product – The brands we associate to a product or service we can buy, e.g. "iPod".

Company – The brands we associate to a company we can buy from, e.g. "Apple".

Personality – The brands we associate to Key People of Influence who represent companies and products, e.g. "Steve Jobs".

The original conversation around branding started with just "product branding". We saw with some of the earliest brands like "Coca-Cola", "Hoover" and "Marlboro" products that were so strong they built multinational companies around them. These companies shared the same name and brand identity as their product; no one knew or cared who the CEO, founder or inventor was.

The second layer to come along was when companies became more complex and started selling multiple products. The separation of "product brands" and "company brands" emerged. McDonald's was known as the *company* that sold *products* like Big Macs, McShakes and McHappy Meals. General Electric, 3M and LG started producing many product ranges and had both strong product as well as company brands. People wanted to know who the company was behind the products; but still didn't expect to know much about the people.

More recently we've seen the emergence of the third type of brand: the "Key Person of Influence brand" or "personality brand". Early adopters like "Nike" used personality brands like "Michael Jordan" to sell their "product brands" like "Air Jordan" shoes. We saw Steve Jobs powering Apple's products like Mac, iPod and iPad. Richard Branson's much-loved personality powered Virgin's company brand from the music industry into completely new products like trains, planes and mobile phones.

With the ubiquitous presence of social media, the personality brand is arguably the most powerful brand to drive your business. If people like and trust you, they will buy the things you represent. And as a small business, it is certainly far easier to compete with big businesses by building a personality brand rather than going up against their established product and company brands as an also-ran.

Australia's John Simmonds built Aussie Home Loans from scratch into a multi-billion dollar mortgage provider. The Australian public had grown used to seeing ads for major banks that all looked the same – faceless, clichéd, typical. Then along came Simmonds, staring straight into the camera, talking to you as the founder and CEO of the company and making a direct promise, "at Aussie, we'll save you".

No one in Australia had ever seen the CEO of a bank making promises to them. No one even knew who the CEO of their bank was. Simmonds' personality brand captured a lot of business in an industry that was sewn up by some of the world's biggest banks.

Consumers want to know who the face behind the sometimes seemingly faceless business is. They don't just want to know the founder or the CEO; they also want to know about the engineers, the leaders and the people who work in the company at a ground level.

Progressive brands like Deloitte and Coutts & Co are responding to these trends. They let their team write blogs, publish articles and speak at conferences; they wear their people proudly on their sleeve rather than hiding them away. Brands like these have discovered it's a lot cheaper to encourage their leaders to build personality brands rather than to find and pay people who already have celebrity status.

Most big companies don't do this yet, which gives small businesses an advantage in building a powerful personality brand. They can easily produce videos, give talks, and write books and blogs. While they may be small, they can look big online.

A small business will never be able to compete with a big business when it comes to company branding or branding. And while big businesses will get better at building personality brands in the future, this is the place that a small business can outperform the bigger players – at least for the time being. As an additional benefit, a business leader who builds a personality brand will attract opportunities beyond the life of any particular business. Industries may change; but key people of influence keep attracting great deals.

I recently spoke to a successful entrepreneur who sold his company for several million dollars but had failed to build any personality brand alongside the business brand. He divulged to me that he felt like he was starting from scratch after the sale, because no one really knew who he was outside his industry and as part of his exit deal he wasn't permitted to contact the people who DID know him.

Conversely, I know of CEOs and leaders who have a long list of opportunities coming their way because they've built a personality brand alongside their business. They attract great opportunities where they are and will continue to do so after they move on to their next venture. When you think of your business, build three brands – your company brand, your product brand and your personality brand.

After you've decided upon the Key Person of Influence, you must now recruit the other vital members of your CDE team. A key person of influence might have some clout but they certainly can't pull off a victory all on their own.

ROLE 2: HEAD OF SALES AND MARKETING

A great sales and marketing person is worth their weight in gold. Throw them into a networking function and they will walk out with warm leads. Give them some warm leads and they will come back the next day with orders. Give them a list of existing clients and they will produce referrals from them. Three things matter to this person – leads, sales, referrals. Everything else is merely a distraction.

A quality sales person transforms your campaigns. I would go so far as to say it's impossible to run campaigns profitably without great sales follow up. When I launched my first company, I was incredibly lucky that my best friend Glen Carlson just so happened to be one of the best sales people in the world and came to create the business with me. To this day, I've never encountered a better mind for insightful, struggle-free sales strategy.

In those early days, I would focus all my efforts into running powerful campaigns every month and generating a lot of buzz and attraction. Glen would make sure we never let a sale slip through the cracks. He made 50+ calls a day, he followed up with people when he said he would, developed scripts that told our story perfectly and then rehearsed them and delivered them. If I gave him a list of 100 hot leads he would give me back 30+ completed sales. The business grew into a seven-figure enterprise in its first year largely because of Glen's prowess on a sales appointment.

Contrast that with most startups that struggle for their first few years. Most of the time, the founder is the only one selling. Rather than building a great product, constructing an effective campaign or doing a breakthrough partnership, they spend their time chasing up sales. Pretty soon they are not effective at sales or growing the business.

There's no point building that awesome landing page or recording that brilliant video if you don't have top sales people. All of those leads will go cold without someone following them up. Your CDE Team needs one person to be accountable for sales and marketing activities.

If you don't have this person, hire them today. Maybe you'll need to ask them to do a commission-only trial period to begin with. Give them 250 warm leads and see what comes back; a good sales person will create more money from 250 leads than the cost of hiring and retaining them.

Remember, you're not going to succeed as a Campaign Driven Enterprise without great sales people. It's unlikely you'll ever become oversubscribed no matter how good your product or how recognized your brand. Remember what we said earlier – big brands like Google, Apple, BMW, Ferrari, HSBC, CitiBank, Virgin, Coca-Cola, Microsoft, Rolex, Omega, Disney all have sales people and training programmes. They are constantly on the lookout for good sales recruits and they all pay their sales people healthy incomes. They have the most valuable brands on earth and they still need sales professionals. So does your CDE Team.

MARKETING TOOLS

Marketing a business is about having access to the right marketing assets. Without these assets you can't expect a person to be able to generate leads for your sales people.

Your marketing team will need to develop these key assets:

Approved copy and images – A marketing person needs to have access to an approved marketing message that is *written down*. They also need access to an image library that represents the brand. A great marketing person can turn this content and imagery into compelling materials but they need you and your company to provide the starting point.

Approved content – The content could include articles, reports, case studies, ideas, recipes, stories, examples, and the like. This could take the form of audio, video or written content. The marketing person can then use this in a hundred different ways to help drive leads.

Lead capture systems – The marketing person will need a system for capturing and storing the data of people who are responsive to the marketing materials. Regardless of whether you use an automated online or an old-school phone system, you need to know who's interested and where they came from.

Measurement benchmarks – Your marketing person needs to know what an allowable cost per lead, allowable cost per sale and an allowable budget all are for testing ideas. If they don't have these benchmarks, they will either become paralysed by fear or go rogue with overactivity.

SALES TOOLS

We mentioned earlier that sales conversations are not merely chit-chat; a sales person needs tools. To be clear, you need to develop these five sales tools for your sales person:

Script – This should be a scripted conversation plan that a sales person can rehearse and perfect. Contrary to what you hear, great sales people *do* use scripts.

Brochure – We live in a digital world, and every company should keep their valuable stuff online. However, there's one important document that has to be in print: your brochure. I don't care if your business is the next Google or Facebook: your sales people need printed brochures. These documents are the glue that holds face-to-face sales conversations together. The mere act of creating a brochure will get your CDE Team aligned to the commercial value of your offering. A good brochure should tell the story of the product, the philosophy behind its creation, the key attributes, the benefits and advantages the product brings. It should talk about the key people who are involved, have case studies and testimonials from users as well as expert opinions and external validation.

Diagram – Your sales people need a diagram that visually depicts the value you offer. It should be something they can easily draw on a napkin and something that creates a story about why your business is valuable. In fact, the diagram should be so simple and powerful that your customers can draw it for *their* friends after seeing it once.

Sign-up form – Your sales people need a physical and a digital form that they can fill in when they reach an agreement with a client. This form signifies the client details, such as how they intend to pay for their products and services. I've met many sales people who have won business but not "signed it up" on the spot, only to watch it go cold later that same week. A sign-up form serves as a powerful marker that indicates that all parties have reached an agreement and we are moving forward together.

Term sheet – A term sheet accompanies a sign-up form and has all the details of what clients are signing up for and the conditions that have been reached. Either party can go back to the term sheet and see exactly what was agreed.

In the same way you can't expect results from a photographer who has no equipment or a dentist who has no instruments, you can't expect a sales person to deliver the results without these tools.

ROLE 3: HEAD OF OPERATIONS

There's a measure that your business needs to know about called "Net Promoter Score" or NPS. Put simply, it's the score your customers would rate you when asked "How likely are you to recommend this business to someone like yourself?" Believe it or not, this one measure is the most highly correlated score for predicting whether your business is going to grow and be profitable.

Research suggests that if the average score is less than 7 out of 10, you've got no chance at growing your business or becoming profitable in the long term. If you score highly, your business has a future.

This is why your head of operations needs to live or die by this number. They need to go to bed thinking about it, wake up thinking about it and spend all day doing what they can to improve it.

Consider how much this score implies. Scoring well indicates that you targeted the right sort of person, set the right expectations, delivered upon them and then exceeded those expectations with unexpected goodness.

The head of operations has to police this score. They have to make sure the marketing and sales teams are setting the right expectations, and that customers get what they wanted – and then get some more on top of that. They have to engineer a way of doing all of this using as much automation and systemization as possible.

They need to believe at their core that every dollar saved has the power to further delight their clients and thus improve that score.

I'm fortunate to be in business with Marcus Ubl. Like Glen Carlson, he's a childhood friend who just happens to be world-class in business. Marcus has a strength for operations. His innovation comes in the form of improving processes and delivering value more consistently and more efficiently than yesterday. Provided sales are flowing, he's able to make the necessary adjustments to improve the experience for clients. I was fortunate that Marcus came to join Glen and me very early on in our business journey. He allowed us to go from making just over $1m in sales to just over $10m in sales because he was able to refine and optimize performance.

Operations people deliver value to customers. They usually aren't the best sales people, because they easily go into "solutions mode" rather than "sales mode". But provided the operations person has paid-up customers to work with, they will be a vital member of the team.

I've hinted before that the one measure that ops people need to focus on is NPS. After that they need to be creative in how to improve it.

There are four areas to focus on here:

Build a better product – A brilliant product will return a great result for Net Promoter Score. If it solves a problem better than anyone expected, then it's going to be hot. A great ops person will always want to improve the product, and it will never be good enough for them. If you let them tinker, they will go above and beyond good judgment to make the product better.

Build a better system of delivery – A great product becomes too expensive if the system of delivery is inefficient. The value you offer is the end result; but inefficiency in how you deliver that pushes costs up, and passes them along to customers or shareholders. Either way, the business is at risk if the systems are sloppy.

Change the target market – If you try to sell a Ferrari to family of five, you will have a low NPS score. The product is world-class, but it's not right for a large family; they would be a lot happier with a sedan. Likewise, if your product is presented to the wrong market, you'll score low on the NPS. The ops person needs to give feedback to the marketing person about the types of people who are loving the product – and those who aren't.

Change the expectations – Expectations are created by marketing and sales people, product packaging, and product delivery or through the client on board-ing process. A good ops person is always on the lookout for the expectations that have been set for the clients. They either need to deliver upon those expectations, or make sure people aren't setting those expectations too high in the first place. For example, if a sales person is making preposterous claims in order to win a sale, the ops person needs to nip it in the bud.

ROLE 4: HEAD OF FINANCE AND REPORTING

For some strange reason, a lot of people see the finance role as boring, dull or even *optional*. Perhaps some people have been burned by a low performer in this role and they now miss the bigger picture, but the finance and reporting role is there to help steer the campaign towards a profitable result. The right person is on the hunt to unlock cash from the operation. They will actively seek access to investment, loans, grants and discounts. They will establish better terms with suppliers, finding ways to get a bulk discount on extended payment terms with added service.

They know that every dollar they unlock creates a bigger opportunity for the business. They walk tall knowing that they are resourcing the whole team and making the impossible possible. Contrary to what many people seem to think, a great finance person isn't ruining the party; they are making the party possible. They are ahead of the game and looking to find ways to get the cash that's needed. They feed information back to the team about what's working and what's not working. They tell the sales person that they are just three sales away from hitting a personal best. They tell the Key Person of Influence that a new milestone has been achieved and they can talk about it when doing deals. They communicate to the ops person that they are spending thousands on non-essential printed materials, and that a digital solution would save them £754 a month on average.

A great finance and reporting person prepares reports that will attract investment and finance. They can tell the team if a campaign was profitable on the day that it finished. This person is hands-on, proactive and has the same spark and drive as the rest of the team. And it's critical for the rest of the team to recognize and foster their talent. It's often the case that all the glory goes to the sales person or the Key Person of Influence. Be sure to celebrate the finance person's achievements, too. High-five them when they cut unnecessary costs. Buy them a bottle of champagne when they secure that overdraft or improve supplier terms.

The finance person should be focused on:

Fast reporting – Give the team the information they need to improve the business. Let them know where small costs have added up, inform them of the expense that produces poor results, give them timely indications of a success or a failure.

Better supplier terms – All good finance people know that if suppliers give better terms, a company's cash position improves tremendously. And the difference between 14-day payment terms and 30-day payment terms can be sink or swim for a small business. If a 5% discount can be arranged, that often goes straight to the bottom line.

Collections – There's no point having a pile of order forms on the desk and no money in the bank. The finance person needs to hustle and get those sales paid up fast. Don't let the cash position of the business slip; if people are paying slow, get on the phone and talk that money across the line.

Access to finance or investment – If the campaigns are working, then you must get ready to expand. It's only a matter of time before the team will want to ramp things up and they will need to attract investment, get a loan or unlock a bigger budget in order to do so. It's the finance person's job to make sure they have the supporting documents to make it happen.

You're ready. Let's go!

You only need to start with this small team of four people who have an aligned vision to become oversubscribed to run successful campaigns. You'll need to apply the principles we talked about at the beginning of this book and work the Campaign Driven Enterprise method.

Keep improving. Keep getting creative. Keep having fun. Most of all, keep your eye on the prize.

Business isn't *inherently* fun. A lot of people experience pain, humiliation, heartbreak and despair as a result of being in business. It can be lonely, frustrating and can suck the life out of you as it drags on over the years.

The dream people are sold is that business is a barrel of laughs. Being an entrepreneur is a path to freedom and adventure. I can tell you that most business people I meet aren't living the dream. But the successful ones I know have something in common: they are oversubscribed.

They have more opportunities than they know what to do with. They have more customers than they can handle. They have investors lining up. They can pick and choose their next adventure with all the options open. They enjoy the stress of being spoilt for choice rather than being out of options.

Being oversubscribed is the gateway to enjoying business. Get yourself into that position and surf the wave.

I want to hear your story. I want to know what you did with this material. I'd love to see your results, check out your campaigns and meet your CDE team. I want to hear about how you live differently after being oversubscribed.

Most of all, I challenge you to really make something big of yourself and your business. Don't just do this stuff for the money; do it for a deeper reason, to make a difference and to give back.

During the industrial revolution, an entrepreneur solved problems related to consumption. People had so many unmet needs for food, shelter, clothing, finance, transport and communications. The people who met these needs amassed great wealth during this time. In that age, entrepreneurs who could get people to consume would be rewarded with a life few people could dream of and wealth beyond measure.

We now live in a world where most people in the Western world have *too much* stuff. We have so much food, clothing, shelter, transport, communications and finance that we're overloaded! The only unmet need people seem to have nowadays is for more storage. And these possessions don't even make us happy anymore; in fact, many people fantasize about living lighter. I know millionaires who are perfectly happy living most of their lives with only two suitcases!

Future entrepreneurs will solve problems of contribution. They will create ways for people to contribute more. The "ALS Ice Bucket Challenge" gave people a silly way to contribute to a cause. Crowd funding platforms are giving people a chance to fund other people's dreams. My business really took off when we focused on helping people to develop and achieve a deeper personal mission.

I believe the entrepreneurs who can unlock the value of contribution will be rewarded greatly now and in the future. These are the individuals who will have influence, travel, adventure and wealth beyond measure. They will be the ones who look back at their life with a smile on their face rather than the pain of regret.

Redefine what entrepreneurship means to you. Rather than focusing on creating new things for people to buy, make it about creating new things for people to get involved in and contribute to. Use what you've learned in this book to make the most of your time here on Earth.

A few trips around the sun. That's all we get. On average, you'll get about 80; maybe if you're lucky you'll get 100. Some people are given a lot less. We really don't know how many more we will get for sure. Many people worry about making an impact in that time, or about their legacy.

But really, no one ever gets to know their legacy. No one can plan it, orchestrate it and/or claim theirs is better or more impactful than anyone else.

Vincent Van Gogh went to his grave believing he was nothing more than a madman and a failed artist. He will never know that his gallery in Amsterdam is one of the most visited in the world or that his art hangs in the National Gallery alongside DaVinci.

Dr Erasmus Darwin was a great inventor, doctor and humanitarian. He would have believed that his greatest achievements were his own and would never have known that his grandson Charles would advance his basic theories around the idea of evolution and write a book that would change the way we see ourselves as a species.

The mother and father of scientist Marie Curie made enormous sacrifices so that their daughter might go to university. They would never know that she would win two Nobel Prizes for her work in physics and chemistry and impact billions of lives. If you asked them whether all the hard work and sacrifice was worth it, they may have harboured doubts.

But no matter their legacy, every person plays an important role on this planet. We must view all success in a broader context rather than in isolation. If humanity is a rich tapestry, some people are on show and are an obvious feature on that tapestry. However, their very existence depends on every other thread that is weaving the masterpiece in place.

There are people in my life who influenced me greatly who have no idea just how much they did. I also know that many of them are not known or famous in any way; some of them don't even know who I am. But I was influenced by their books or their talks. I hope that my work is having a positive impact in ways I'm not aware of.

Sometimes being a good friend, sending a thoughtful letter, showing compassion to a stranger or sharing an authentic moment can spark a chain of events that impacts the world.

My challenge to you is to put down this book and to go make the most of your few trips around the sun.

Being oversubscribed isn't a marketing exercise for me. It's about playing full out so that I can impact the most number of people and I can create something special.

I don't want you to be oversubscribed so you make a little bit of extra money or shave off a little bit of spare time. My vision is that you use the ideas in this book to make a difference to your life and to the lives of others.

When I'm writing, I imagine you putting down this book and going off to create something astonishing. I imagine some of these chapters calling you to create your very best work.

Our lives are barely a second in the grand scheme of things. Yet in that time we are afforded an opportunity to do the best we can with what we have and trust the process that something good will come of it all. In any case, if you go out to create something of value you will barely fathom the ways you impact the world just by being here for those precious few laps around the sun.

ONE LAST THING: THE CHAPTER I WRESTLED WITH

There's a chapter in this book that almost didn't make it in. Not because it wasn't good enough to be in the book but because I felt scared to give it away. It's an idea that has made me a lot of money and saved me a lot of time. Before I knew this particular idea, I lost a fortune in time, effort and income. Most people don't know this idea and I can see them struggle as a result.

I almost didn't put this chapter in the book. I felt uneasy sharing it so freely. I'm normally very open when it comes to sharing ideas, however, I know just how hard I worked for it and I would hate for it to be devalued.

As with any idea, you can only unleash its value through implementation. You might have recognized the power of this simple idea, but if you don't do anything with it, it's completely worthless to you. I would have shared it for nothing.

Maybe you know exactly which chapter I'm talking about – or sadly, you might have missed it. You could have skimmed right over it and not even realized what a gem it was. That too would be unfortunate for us both.

I'm not going to say which chapter I wrestled with. I'm going to leave it for you to discover on your own and then to let me know when you know it for sure (tweet me your thoughts – @danielpriestley).

If you re-read the book, you might spot it. You might suddenly sit up and think "Now that's an idea that would be transformational for my business!"

My challenge to you is to then do something with it. Don't let it slip away. Don't bury it in your thoughts; go and act on it. Go and create something new.

If indeed you've found the idea in that chapter, you'll have saved yourself a fortune in trial and error. You'll be on your way to making more money, having more fun and being more in control of your business and your future.

I hope you find it.

ACKNOWLEDGEMENTS

I'm a lucky man – oversubscribed with wonderful mentors, supporters, investors, partners, friends and family.

I'd especially like to thank my business partners and two best friends Marcus Ubl and Glen Carlson. Most of the stories in the book are only possible because of their brilliance.

I'd like to thank Jeremy Harbour for being a great friend, advisor and investor. Thanks Mike Carter and Miles Frost for being brilliant business minds and easy-going gentlemen.

A special acknowledgment to the dynamic global team of leaders and investors – Richard Burch, Oona Collins, Sam Elam, Andrew Griffiths, Callum Lang, Steven Harbour, Topher Morrison, Steven Oddy, Mike Reid, Darren Shirlaw and Keiron Sparrowhawk.

I'd also like to thank the entire KPI community around the world for providing an ongoing dose of inspiration and energy that seems to get stronger every day.

Thanks to Andrew Priestley for being a wonderful dad and for bringing my books to life with cartoons. Thanks to my wonderful mother Diane Priestley for being so supportive, understanding and inspiring. Thanks to my amazing, wonderful sister Justine.

A very special thank you to my perfect partner in life and creativity, Aléna (while I was busy writing this book, you were magically making our wonderful little boy! Thank you xxx).

ABOUT THE AUTHOR

Daniel Priestley is a best-selling author and award-winning entrepreneur.

He founded his first company in 2002 in Australia, at the age of twenty-one. Before he was twenty-five, he and his business partners had grown a national business turning over several million dollars.

In 2006, Daniel moved from Australia to launch a new venture in London. Arriving with only a suitcase and a credit card, Daniel set up a new venture and grew it to seven-figure revenues in less than two years. In the process, he became a leading figure in his industry and had the opportunity to be mentored personally by some of the world's top entrepreneurs and leaders.

Daniel's entrepreneurial career has included starting, building, buying, financing and selling businesses. He's now regarded as one of the world's top professional speakers on business and entrepreneurship.

He is well known for making a product oversubscribed. Daniel's has sold out large theatre auditoriums, run international campaigns and reinvented products to see sales increase exponentially. He's been involved in raising millions of dollars growth capital for early stage companies.

Today, Daniel works with his lifelong friends and business partners to build a global entrepreneurship and leadership programme. He is also active in fund-raising for charity and working with the leadership teams.

Daniel is also the author of the books *Entrepreneur Revolution* and *Key Person of Influence*.

THE OVERSUBSCRIBED
WORKSHOP

Ready to apply what you've read here...?

Every year Daniel runs a number of two-day workshops, offering intensive coaching on the Oversubscribed principles and becoming a Campaign Driven Enterprise. He is also a guest speaker at conferences and events for growing businesses.

So if you are truly determined to get your customers lining up then email **oversubscribed@entrevo.com** to find out more.

PLUS.....

Daniel is giving away **free tickets** or samples of his new products to everyone who reviews this book!

Daniel Priestley's company Entrevo regularly hosts events, webinars, discussions, pitching competitions and networking (online and in the 'real world'). To see what's coming up visit **www.entrevo.com**.

So, if you would like to review this book, we will reward you for taking the time to do so. Here's how:

1. Write a review of this book

2. Post it on Amazon, iTunes Bookstore, your blog, your Facebook page, or get it published in another publication

3. Send a link or a screenshot to reviews@entrevo.com

4. You will be sent free tickets to upcoming events or receive samples of new products and services from Entrevo (depending on where you are and what we have going on at the time)

Thanks for reading **OVERSUBSCRIBED!**